The British Film Business

The British Film Business

Bill Baillieu
and
John Goodchild

JOHN WILEY & SONS, LTD

Other Wiley Editorial Offices

John Wiley & Sons, Inc., 605 Third Avenue,
New York, NY 10158-0012, USA

Wiley-VCH Verlag GmbH, Pappelallee 3,
D-69469 Weinheim, Germany

John Wiley & Sons Australia, Ltd, 33 Park Road, Milton,
Queensland 4064, Australia

John Wiley & Sons (Asia) Pte Ltd, 2 Clementi Loop #02-01,
Jin Xing Distripark, Singapore 129809

John Wiley & Sons (Canada) Ltd, 22 Worcester Road,
Rexdale, Ontario M9W 1L1, Canada

Library of Congress Cataloging-in-Publication Data

A Library of Congress record has been applied for

British Library Cataloguing in Publication Data

A catalogue record for this book is available from the British Library

ISBN 0-471-49918-8
Typeset in 11/13pt RotisSerif by Footnote Graphics, Warminster, Wiltshire
Printed and bound in Great Britain by TJ International Ltd, Padstow, Cornwall
This book is printed on acid-free paper responsibly manufactured from sustainable
forestation, for which at least two trees are planted for each one used for paper production.

The image is almost picaresque — the sharp and hardened salesman leading the well-intentioned but bumbling and naive Sunday School teacher along the dangerous Babylonian corridors of Soho film-land as the various rogues and spivs, skulking in doorways, leap out and importune Rank, demanding money for shady film projects.

Geoffrey Macnab
J. Arthur Rank and the British Film Industry

Contents

Contents

Contents

Introduction

'The most striking fact about the British film industry is that it is not British.' So wrote Ernest Betts in *The Film Business* (1973), arguing that the industry was 'as much American as British, if not more so'. For the past 80 years British producers, exhibitors and distributors have operated in the shadow of Hollywood; and that shadow has had considerable substance. The competitive edge gained by the American industry during the First World War was consolidated in the 1920s via a network of distributors in London; by the end of that decade those distributors were backing 'British' films to fulfil their quota requirements. Later, strategic shareholdings were acquired in leading exhibitors such as Gaumont-British, Odeon and ABPC.

The importance of the British market was recognised by Hollywood at a very early stage, and whatever forms of protectionism have been introduced by governments to assist the domestic trade, they have invariably failed. This book is written in the context of that American 'colonisation'. The lack of production finance that has hampered British film-makers over the decades is contrasted with the marked success of exhibitors and distributors in attracting capital from institutional and private investors. The role of government is discussed: a consistent failure to understand the nature of the industry has often led to badly drafted legislation and unsatisfactory initiatives.

In fairness, a general lack of agreement among the trade bodies has occasionally precipitated 'independent' government action such as the Cinematograph Films Act 1927, which was intended to support a struggling industry against American competition. The act fixed a yearly quota of British films which cinemas were obliged to show and distributors had to offer for hire. The act led to the emergence of 'quota quickies': low-budget productions of inferior quality, often funded by American companies, that had little success at the box office. True, they provided employment, but the net effect was to give British films a bad name at home and abroad.

In the aftermath of the Second World War, Britain faced a balance of payments crisis, and in 1947 the Labour government imposed a 75% *ad valorem* duty on imported films. The aim was to limit dollar expenditure. However, the policy backfired when Hollywood suspended the export of its films and boycotted British productions. Within months a compromise was reached which limited dollar remittances to the US and allowed non-returnable earnings to be invested in 'British' films.

Problems have often arisen when governments have given the industry direct or indirect subsidies. In 1948 the President of the Board of Trade, Harold Wilson, established the National Film Finance Corporation (NFFC). Its aim was to support British production via a system of loans. There were initial triumphs like *The Third Man* and *The Happiest Days of Your Life* and, until it was wound up by the Conservative government in 1985, the NFFC had supported 780 features as well as many television films and shorts. However, there were numerous box-office failures, and out of total loans of £43 million granted by the NFFC only £21.7 million was repaid. A poor record in financial terms, but without NFFC backing, British film production might well have collapsed by the 1950s.

The Eady Plan proved to be a more robust subsidy scheme until it too was abolished in 1985. Named after the Treasury official who created it, the plan was introduced in 1950 and involved the raising of seat prices in cinemas and the payment of one farthing for every ticket sold into the British Film Production Fund. In exchange, the exhibitors benefited from lower entertainments tax rates. Adjustments were made in 1951 and it was estimated that the scheme would raise around £12.5 million from cinema-goers, of which an extra £2.3 million would go to producers. Eady money was paid out on the basis of the box-office receipts of British films that qualified for the quota. So the more successful the producer, the more Eady money he received. The definition of a British film also worked against the intention to promote new talent, as Hollywood producers could use the system to their own advantage and qualify for Eady money by financing 'British' productions. The basis of distribution came under regular attack, usually from independent producers who resented the fact that successful films received a 'bonus' in the form of a larger subsidy.

The mid 1980s witnessed what appeared to be an exciting renaissance in the British film industry when Goldcrest Films burst onto the scene. A string of critical and box-office hits were produced before it collapsed and was bought out at a bargain price – a catastrophe for the independent production sector because it alienated investors and prompted references to the slump of the late 1930s.

However, towards the end of the 1990s, when Britain was again seeing an explosion of talent and home-produced box-office hits, the National Lottery and the Labour government channelled money via the Arts Council into a number of British production companies. It was an unsuccessful strategy, both commercially and artistically, with millions of pounds spent on films, many of which have never been screened. However, the launch of the Film Council under Alan Parker in 2000 does offer some cause for optimism. There is an opportunity to restructure production on a root-and-branch basis, with greater investment in project and script development, training and commercially viable screenplays. The Film Council has £150 million to spend over a three-year period and Parker has said that he also intends to shake up film distribution, marketing and merchandising.

After decades of half-hearted meddling by successive governments and a fragmented industry that has suffered from poor distribution and insufficient investment, a coordinated commercial and funding strategy is now possible. The Film Council will have to absorb the marketing lessons of Hollywood and the changes that the internet is bringing to distribution techniques and viewing habits. Most of all, it will need to move quickly in a ruthlessly competitive world or the British film business will become a cottage industry, occasionally making a bright, popular garment but unable to sustain a vigorous and creative production line.

Our thanks are due to everyone who has helped in the writing of this book. In particular, we are indebted to Sandra Vanzanten and Janet Andreasen for invaluable assistance with the manuscript; Mary Daws of the Policy Studies Institute for providing important research material; and Claire Fowler of the Financial Times for guiding us through that newspaper's archives. We also received generous help and encouragement from members of the British Film Institute and the staff at both the Guildhall Library and the Newington Road Reference Library.

Finally, we must thank Sally Smith, Benjamin Earl and the team at John Wiley for their patience and dedication in seeing this book into production.

Bill Baillieu
& John Goodchild
April 2002

CHAPTER 1

The Early Years: 1896–1914

The birth of the commercial cinema in Britain can be dated precisely – 20 February 1896. On that day the Lumière brothers' films were shown at the Royal Polytechnic Institute in London. Perhaps appropriately, the programme was introduced by Monsieur Trewey, a magician and friend of the Lumières. An admission charge was made and the short films – under one minute in duration – included 'Workers Leaving the Lumière Factory', 'Congress of Photographic Studies' and 'Watering the Gardener'. The public response was enthusiastic, and in March Trewey took the Lumière *Cinématographé* to the Empire Music Hall in Leicester Square for a series of nightly performances that continued for 18 months.

These films, often forming part of the bill in a music hall, were regarded as no more than a novelty by both the audiences and their producers. Few, if any, appreciated the potential and, referring to his invention, Auguste Lumière is quoted as saying 'it can be exploited for a certain time as a scientific curiosity but, apart from that, it has no commercial future whatsoever' (Bardèche and Brasillach 1938).

ORIGINS

Before the first public exhibition of films in England and France (the *Cinématographé* had been premiered in Paris in December 1895), scientists, inventors and photographers had been struggling for many years with the problem of how to achieve moving pictures. Optical toys, such as the zoetrope and the phenakistoscope, represented early experiments, and the magic lantern, which had been invented in the seventeenth century, became very popular during the Victorian era. During this period significant advances occurred in the United States and France. In 1879 Eadweard Muybridge, an Englishman living in America, took a series of 24 photographs, using 24 cameras, of a trotting horse. When 'projected' via his zoopraxiscope the illusion of a horse in motion was created. At about the same time, in France, Étienne-Jules Marey became interested in the possibility of photographing birds in flight and designed a camera – in fact a 'photographic gun' – which recorded the movement of a seagull. In England, William Friese-Greene produced various cameras, though there is little evidence of material filmed by him or shown publicly. But Augustin Le Prince, a Frenchman working in Leeds, had built a single-lens camera-projector in 1888 and was on the point of making adjustments to accommodate the new celluloid film when he disappeared on a trip to France.

The real breakthrough came in the United States as a result of the work done by Thomas Edison and a Scotsman, W.K.L. Dickson, who had emigrated to America in 1879. Having put the finishing touches to his phonograph, Edison directed his attention to the film. By 1892 the collaboration with Dickson had resulted in a camera which took pictures at a rate of 46 per second and used celluloid film. To exhibit the films they devised a kinetoscope, a viewing cabinet or peepshow operated by a coin-in-the-slot mechanism. Its drawback was that only one person at a time could watch the films. Edison regarded his kinetoscope as a novelty and, despite its popularity in the United States and Europe, he failed to patent the machine in England.

This oversight led to Robert W. Paul, a scientific instrument maker in London, copying the kinetoscope and successfully marketing it in Britain and overseas. Paul also built a camera and projector during 1895 and a public demonstration was held at the Royal Institution on 28 February 1896 – eight days after the Lumière exhibition. Another Englishman, Birt Acres, constructed a combined camera and projector, and in 1895 he filmed the Derby, the Oxford and Cambridge Boat Race and, at the invitation of the German government, the opening of the Kiel Canal. These early newsreels were shown at the Royal Photographic Society in January 1896.

Edison's kinetoscope inspired the Lumière brothers in France. They owned a photographic works and their experiments reached fruition with the *Cinématographé*. Using the same film as Edison but with a single round perforation, it was presented at the Grand Café in Paris on 28 December 1895.

EXHIBITION

The events that occurred in the winter of 1895–96 laid the foundations of the British film industry, and Robert W. Paul was the central figure at this embryonic stage. His first commercial presentation, featuring such films as 'Rough Seas at Dover' and 'An Indian War Dance' took place at the Olympia in March 1896, and in the same month he began a residency at the Alhambra, Leicester Square. Such was the success of his theatrograph that the show continued until 1900. (An early coup was Paul's newsreel of Persimmon winning the Derby in 1896; the film was shown at the Alhambra on the night of the race.)

The music hall was the first home of the cinema and soon short films became part of the programme in halls throughout the country; but the new attraction quickly reached audiences in more modest venues:

> The Rev Frank Iliff, chaplain to the Lewisham Infirmary, would, on occasions, give a lantern slide lecture to the public and donate the proceeds for the benefit of the men and women of that institution.
>
> On 18 September 1896 at the Lewisham Art Club, he presented a new and rather exciting entertainment with the aid of his 'recently purchased cinematograph'. The *Kentish Mercury* went on to report that 'eight living pictures were thrown upon the screen much to the amazement and delight of those present'. Among the films shown were 'The Waves at Brighton', 'Steamer on the Rhine', 'A Street Scene in Paris', etc. and two comedies. The admission charge of sixpence was donated to the Lewisham Infirmary Christmas Gift Fund. (George 1987, p. v)

Apart from the music hall proprietors, others began to appreciate the financial potential of films; these were the travelling showmen and fairground operators.

The former, who became known as 'town hall' showmen, travelled around the country putting on films in towns and villages and staying until audiences began to wane. Quite often that stay extended over many months and became the basis of the 'picture going' habit. Of more significance, however, was the fairground. As early as 1896 a number of operators, the most prominent of whom was Randall Williams, began to show films on their sites. Williams called his presentation a 'Living Picture Exhibition' and the use of electricity ensured better picture quality than his rivals in the municipal halls. Mobile units were taken to fairs throughout the country and those units could seat up to 800 people. At the Nottingham Goose Fair alone, six separate shows were presented (Low and Manvell 1948, p. 37). This was the pattern of exhibition as the nineteenth century ended, but change was imminent:

> Films were still the small man's business concern in the first years of the century, but this was not to last long. The enthusiasts, the inventors, and the pioneers were soon edged out of the industry by the men who saw there was money to be made out of the exhibition of films to a public made hungry by the excitement of show business. (Manvell 1955, p. 185)

In 1904 Lt Colonel A.C. Bromhead, who was to become chairman of the Gaumont-British Corporation in the late 1920s, opened the Daily Bioscope in Bishopsgate in the City of London. The site was a converted shop, or 'penny gaff', seating about 100 people. Newsreels were the standard fare (PEP 1952, p. 25). Two years later George Hale, an American, opened a 'cinema' in Oxford Street. The premises had also been a shop and the conversion took the form of a railway carriage. The audience sat in the carriage and watched travel films through its windows; and they were charged 6d for the privilege. Soon, 'Hale's Tours' opened in towns and cities throughout England. Their appeal was short-lived, but Hale's idea and its execution prompted other businessmen to convert shops, garages and ice-skating rinks into cinemas. And, 'between 1908 and the first world war a transformation took place. The fixed show, with the specially built picture theatre following hard on its heels, was to draw millions of pounds into the exhibiting side of the industry' (Low 1949, p. 29).

These early cinemas, or 'fixed shows', were comfortable rather than lavish; their aim was to create an atmosphere of elegance and good taste and such names as the Bijou and the Gem were used to underline their owners' search for 'class'. Some of these Bijous were relatively small, seating three hundred or less, but others seated a thousand or more. Programmes frequently had a musical accompaniment in the form of a trio or a pianist. The entrepreneurs had shown sound judgement in assessing the public's growing taste for films, and the opening of the Electric Empire in New Cross, southeast London, illustrates the point:

> Some buildings have a certain style to send one's imagination into instant thoughts of – picture palace! but there would be disappointment for the observer of this apparent little gem. Its origins were far more mundane. It was built before 1900 for a Mr Ransford as part of his then thriving business as a general horse dealer. He vacated the premises in 1908 and the following year, probably only by virtue of its position and simple conversion, was opened for 'living pictures'! Their advertisement in the local press claimed that it was 'the finest and most up-to-date picture theatre in the south of London,' and there would be 'special theatrical effects'; also 'the most refined, instructive and amusing entertainment in the world. Plays without words' etc. Admission prices were 3d and 6d for a reserved seat, and on Sunday 26 September, would be shown 'Gaumont's magnificent production *The Life of Christ*'.
>
> The *Brockley News* for 15 October 1909 reports record attendances on Saturday and Sunday of some 2,000 persons. A new screen was installed by February 1910, many people not being able to gain admittance to the first shows. (George 1987, p. 5)

In 1908 there were just 3 exhibiting companies registered in the United Kingdom with a combined capital of £110,000; by 1914 the number had risen to 1,833 with a total capital of £11.3 million (PEP 1952, p. 26). According to the *Bioscope* of 27 March 1913, the peak was reached in 1910 when there were 295 companies registered with an average capital of £10,000. By 1913, although the number of companies had grown strongly, the average capital was £3,000.

Despite a trend towards single ownership, the pre-war period witnessed the creation of a number of cinema chains. Among these were Electric Theatres (1908), Biograph Theatres (1908) and Provincial Cinematograph Theatres (1909). Electric Theatres was founded with a capital of £50,000 and by 1909 owned 12 theatres (Low 1949, p. 20). In that year it paid a dividend of 40% and planned expansion that would include production and a rental business as well as exhibition. The capital was to be increased to £400,000, but shareholders were wary of the proposal and the company was forcedto expand in a more modest fashion. In 1910 there were 23 theatres in the chain, but by 1914 this had fallen to 17. Dividends also tumbled: from the 1909 peak of 40% to 5% in 1912. The cost of maintaining and improving the theatres was taking its toll on profitability. The history of Electric Theatres is interesting in that its attempt at vertical integration – the combination of production, distribution and exhibition within one company – was the basis of the American domination of world markets in subsequent years.

A similar fate befell Biograph Theatres Ltd, which had five theatres in 1909 and planned to construct another seven. The year 1909 saw dividends of 17.5% paid; by 1912 they had declined to 7.5% (ibid., p. 21). Early optimism was soon overtaken by the reality of managing cinemas that were already outmoded and costly to maintain.

On the other hand, Provincial Cinematograph Theatres Ltd (PCT) flourished and was to play an important role in the development of the Gaumont-British Corporation in the late 1920s. PCT had an initial capital of £100,000 and its aim was to open cinemas in every town with a population in excess of 250,000. In 1911 the company had 8 theatres and by 1914 this figure had reached 18. In 1913 it launched a production company, the London Film Company, and in the same year PCT was quoted on the Stock Exchange, capitalised at £400,000 (ibid., p. 21). Some months before the war, PCT launched Associated Provincial Picture Theatres Ltd, and the combined capital of parent and offspring amounted to almost £1 million. The enlarged group was the first successful example of vertical integration in the British film industry.

By the outbreak of war in 1914, there were 109 circuits in Great

Britain and they accounted for nearly 20% of the cinemas (the total number is estimated at between 3,000 and 4,000 and the *Kinematograph Year Book* for 1915 listed 3,500; the *Bioscope* of June 1914 suggested as many as 7,000). Most of the circuits were small – only three had over 20 cinemas – and ranged from 2 to 29 venues. The smaller circuits tended to be local.

As the number of cinemas grew throughout this period, the owners realised the need for a representative organisation and consequently the Cinematograph Exhibitors' Association (CEA) was formed in 1912. The association's second annual dinner was reported in the *Times* and the chairman, Dr R.T. Jupp, who was managing director of PCT, made some interesting comments on the state of the industry:

> Whereas seven years ago 900 people were employed in the industry, now there were 120,000. There were at present about 5,000 picture theatres in the country and the number of people who paid for admission every week was about 7,000,000. The capital of the industry totalled about £70,000,000 and last year alone about 544 new companies were registered representing a capital of nearly £3,000,000. (*Times*, 4 March 1914)

REGULATION

The growth in the number of cinemas after 1908 led to government intervention on the grounds of public safety. Cinemas were not subject to the same regulations that applied to theatres and music halls and the trade did not object to the Cinematograph Films Act which became law in January 1910. It was known as the Showman's Charter, implying a degree of respectability that the trade had not enjoyed before. The act covered fireproofing, proper ventilation and the like, but it also allowed local authorities to intervene in the running of cinemas on the basis of 'public well-being'. In other words, censorship and the act paved the way for Sunday closing.

The industry was horrified: London cinemas were very successful on Sundays. In 1910 the London County Council brought an action to enforce Sunday closing, but it failed. The argument rumbled on and eventually a compromise was reached in the following year when it was agreed with the exhibitors that Sunday profits would be given to charity. The exhibitors accepted this compromise but did not always comply.

The question of censorship was solved from within the industry. The British Board of Film Censors was formed by the Kinematograph Manufacturers' Association (which had existed since 1906), and its examiners were independent of the trade. The board began operations in January 1913 with the backing of the Home Office and the exhibitors. The exhibitors were particularly enthusiastic because they saw it as deliverance from the arbitrary power of local authorities.

DISTRIBUTION

With the emergence of the first cinema chains, the distribution of films developed into a major business. Initially, the showmen bought films directly from producers such as Robert W. Paul and Cecil Hepworth, who published catalogues of their titles. In addition to the home trade there was a flourishing export market. In fact, some of Paul's catalogues had details in German (Low and Manvell 1948, p. 33). Prices for the export market ranged between 6d and 8d per foot; the home market price settled at 6d.

This pattern of direct sales by the manufacturer to the exhibitor continued for some years, but the film rental trade did develop rapidly. Exhibitors built up stocks of films which they, in turn, rented out to other exhibitors. Among the first companies to specialise in this aspect of the business were Walturdaw and Jury's Imperial Pictures. They hired out 'sets' of films (a complete programme) at what became a standard rate of £2 10s per 1,000 feet per night, and supplied clients such as Keith Prowse and Harrods as well as the Church Mission Halls (ibid., p. 34).

Rental companies bought their films from producers and the situation arose where films were available for purchase and hire concurrently, similar in fact to the sale and hire of videos today. Scores of new films were being released on a weekly basis and the producers began to fear that lower prices would result. In 1906 Pathé, the French company that produced about 20% of all the films shown in

England, reduced its price to 4d a foot. A price war ensued and by 1909 Cricks and Martin had cut their price to 3d. The problem facing the industry was how should the price of a film be determined? Gradually, opinion shifted in the direction of exclusivity: one dealer would handle a particular film and have the 'exclusive' rights in its promotion and exhibition. In 1911 *Princess Clementina*, an exclusive, had a print run of 20 copies as opposed to 395 copies of Hepworth's earlier success, *Rescued by Rover* (1905). The money paid for exclusives quickly rose to staggering heights: *Quo Vadis* was auctioned for £6,700 and *Battle of Waterloo* was sold for £5,000. These films were widely publicised, and reflected the public's growing taste for quality pictures rather than the miscellany of short films that usually constituted the average programme.

Inevitably this change caused resentment, and as early as 1908 the *Bioscope* suggested that rates should be reduced after 'first run' showings and the films finally sold to showmen. But the 'open market' system of distribution did not disappear and in 1914 some 400 exclusives were released as opposed to 6,648 films on the open market (PEP 1952, p. 27).

The public's demand for feature films of greater quality was nurtured, at least partially, by American and French productions. In 1910 France provided 36% of the films released in the UK and the US 28% (Low 1949, p. 33). Britain came a poor fourth with 15% after Italy's 17%. Together with Italy and France, particularly the Pathé Company, Britain was an important exporter of films during the first ten years of the industry's development. But the move towards feature films involved higher production costs and the financial backing was not readily available. The UK was not a sufficiently large market to justify this kind of investment and, even before the outbreak of war, international sales were diminishing as the American industry expanded. As Charles Oakley observed, 'Wall Street was film-minded. The City of London was not' (Oakley 1964, p. 61).

PRODUCTION

Over the ten years following the Lumière brothers' London presentation, thousands of films were made in Britain. Most were relatively short, a minute or two in length, and this remained the pattern for some time. The subject matter was fairly broad, covering topical events, travelogues, comedy, music hall turns and, by around 1904–5, drama. The success of Cecil Hepworth's *Falsely Accused* (1906), which ran for 14 minutes, is a good example of the emerging demand for longer, narrative films. But the most famous film of this time was *Rescued by Rover* (1905), another Hepworth production. It cost £7 13s 9d to make and ran for about 7 minutes (425 feet). Positive prints were sold for £10 12s 6d and, in fact, Hepworth remade the film twice, thereby producing three versions, because he wore out the negative twice (Low and Manvell 1948, p. 108).

There were some dozen production companies operating in this early period, the most important of which were those run by Robert W. Paul and Cecil Hepworth. Paul's Animatograph Works, based in Muswell Hill, was at its peak between 1900 and 1905, when it was producing an average of 50 films a year. The Hepworth Manufacturing Company expanded rapidly from 100 films in 1900 to twice that number in 1906. The Warwick Trading Company, which had been reorganised by Charles Urban in 1898, produced 150 films in that year and by 1903 this had grown to over 500 titles. The company's catalogue was boosted by its considerable overseas staff who sent local material, e.g. European cities and beauty spots, and its total annual output was far greater than any of the other production groups (ibid., p. 25).

The French company Gaumont opened an office in London in 1898 and began by selling imported films and equipment. Soon, however, it started to produce and distribute, becoming 'one of the most important selling agents in the world for both British and foreign film' (ibid., p. 21). Gaumont handled films made by Cecil Hepworth and the Brighton film-makers James Williamson and G.A. Smith. Smith was recalled by Roger Manvell:

> In 1946 I went with my colleague Rachael Low (the historian of the early period of British films) to see one of the pioneers of motion pictures, George Albert Smith, at his house in Brighton. He showed us the little notebooks in which he kept his first accounts. He had been a portrait photographer who in 1897 began to make simple record films of the streets and beaches at

Brighton. The account books showed columns with small amounts in shillings and pence for outlay and receipts during the first months of his work, but he showed us that by 1900 his profit from the sale and exhibition of his films had amounted to £1,800. (Manvell 1955, p. 17)

For around five years, until 1911, British film production went through a period of stagnation. In volume terms, the number of films released did increase, but a high proportion of films exhibited in the cinemas were of French, Italian and American origin. Robert W. Paul returned to scientific instrument making and although Cecil Hepworth continued making 'shorts' at his Walton-on-Thames studios, he eventually set up a distribution company handling foreign films. He recognised that, in the main, these films were superior to British productions and it was a wish to make films of a greater artistic and technical quality that drew him back into production with *Rachel's Sin* (1911). It was commercially successful and prompted others to concentrate on feature-length, one-reel productions, e.g. Barker's *Henry VIII* (also 1911). And the major French company Pathé recognised a business opportunity and began production in Britain at this time.

The main production companies in the immediate pre-war years were those associated with Hepworth, Barker and Dr Jupp. In 1913 the London Film Company was formed with a capital of £40,000. American talent was used on its productions and the first film, *The House of Temperley* (1913), was an instant hit. It concentrated on features and the company was both well managed and well funded.

This brief revival in British production, which was based on longer films, often adaptations of stage plays, could not mask the growing significance of the US industry. Hollywood had targeted Britain as one of its most important markets: it was the centre for international trade and 'the world's clearing house for films' (Street 1997, p. 5). American films were becoming very popular with British audiences and the expansion of the exhibition side of the business after 1908 was an additional attraction for American producers. The money that had backed the exhibitors was not generally forthcoming for production and British films failed to find a reciprocal market in the United States. In fact, 'British inferiority, both commercial and artistic, was openly recognised some years before the war' (Low 1949, p. 133).

In May 1914 two directors of the US company Famous Players, Edwin S. Porter (director of *The Great Train Robbery*) and Hugh Ford, visited London and announced plans for establishing studios in England and France. The outbreak of war put an end to their plans — and possibly those of other American producers — but it did not prevent the inexorable rise of Hollywood as the ultimate force in world markets.

AMERICA

The American film industry had similar beginnings to the British film industry. The showmen and the fairground operators were the early exhibitors of films which were sold rather than hired, and the subjects were simple. But the situation quickly changed. The Edison Company was unable to prevent its patents being copied and in 1908 the ten major US producers and manufacturers combined to form the Motion Picture Patents Company. This 'Trust', as it became known, effectively monopolised the production and exhibition sides of the industry: it charged for the use of its cameras and projectors via a licence fee and in 1910 formed the General Film Company which controlled the distribution of all films in the United States.

The opposition to these developments was led by William Fox, who continued working as an exhibitor, producer and distributor. Other producers who opposed the Trust included Carl Laemmle, the founder of Universal Pictures and the man credited with the growth of the star system in Hollywood. The independent producers used 'stars' in their films and this boosted their popularity with audiences at home and abroad. The films made by the Patents Company members were dull by comparison, and as Europe became involved in the First World War, the litigious battles in the US film industry were drawing to a close. In 1915 the US Federal Court ordered that the Patents Company should be wound up.

During the period of the patents war, Hollywood had become established as the centre of American film-making. But the companies also controlled exhibition and distribution, thus establishing the pattern of vertical integration that would not be attempted in Britain, to any great extent, until the late 1920s. They approached the production and marketing of films as a business, and despite various forms of protectionism introduced by European countries, the American film came to dominate world screens.

CHAPTER 2

The First World War to the Talkies

The British film industry had been correct in its assumption that audiences would grow during the war; in 1917 some 20 million people were visiting the cinema every week (*Bioscope*, 21 March 1918). What the industry had failed to realise was the extent to which American films would dominate British screens.

Hollywood, having emerged from the era of the patents war, was in an ideal position to expand. The First World War had caused the closure of studios in France, Germany and Italy, and after an initial flurry in Britain, production declined. The Americans seized their opportunity and between 1914 and 1916 US film exports almost doubled, with over 50% coming to Britain (PEP 1952, p. 32). When the United States entered the war in 1917 there was a fall in its exports, but by 1920 a strong recovery was under way – 188.5 million feet exported, 25% to the UK (ibid., p. 32). The American industry had taken full advantage of its three-year period of neutrality to create a near monopoly of the world's film market. That position has been maintained to this day.

PRODUCTION

In the years immediately preceding the First World War there had been a revival in British film production. The net result was that in 1914 around 25% of films shown in UK cinemas were British (against 15% in 1910), and in the early days of the war this trend continued, with the active encouragement of the government. This led to news-reels of the war becoming an integral part of cinema programmes, as well as short films prompting audiences to 'save coal'. A successful documentary, *The Battle of the Somme* (1916), raised some £30,000 for the war effort (*Bioscope*, 12 October 1916).

British producers like Cecil Hepworth and Will Barker continued to make films with the emphasis on feature-length adaptations of plays and successful novels. Gaumont opened a studio at Shepherd's Bush in 1914, at an estimated cost of £30,000, and in 1915 opened Lime Grove, an even bigger complex. However, Gaumont's output was meagre during this time, as was that of the other leading French company, Pathé, whose Alexandra Palace studios were requisitioned by the government (Oakley 1964, p. 67). New companies emerged, but they were generally small and undercapitalised (the average registered capital was £10,000). The largest studios were at Twickenham – owned by Dr Jupp's London Films – and the use of American talent on their early productions resulted in higher artistic and technical standards. But many of their directors and performers left as the war progressed and by 1918 the studios were being hired out to other film-makers.

The tide of American films and their growing popularity, particularly the Chaplin comedies, caused concern to the British government. The outlay on American titles was a worry at a time when saving foreign currency was a cornerstone of war policy and government action took the form of an import tax on film stock. This was introduced in the 1915 Budget and the measure was expected to raise £400,000 a year. The tax varied on the type of stock involved: 8d a foot on negative, 1d on positive and ½d on raw stock (Low 1950, p. 111).

The industry immediately recognised that the main areas affected would be production and printing, especially for the re-export trade. The Kinematograph Film Makers' Association (KMA), which had been formed in 1907, lobbied aggressively for reductions in the levels of tax and by the end of the year some concessions were made. However, although this had the effect of virtually ending the re-export business, the producers were relatively unscathed since the number of films made after 1916 slumped dramatically.

It is perhaps ironic that during the war British films appeared under 'at least eighty brands and trademarks' (ibid., p. 48). Although the producers realised that the possibilities of export would be limited, they believed an opportunity existed to capture the home market. Until 1916 output grew and films also increased in length – the feature film as we know it today was developing rapidly. But the overall quality was indifferent and the industry was shackled by a shortage of capital at a time when production costs were rising: £4,000 was reckoned to be the average cost of a film throughout the war (ibid., p. 53).

As well as Gaumont, other firms emerged from the renting sector to begin production at this time, including Ideal, Butcher's and Stoll. But in 1918 there were only two public companies involved in British production: the London Film Company, capital £120,000, and Broadwest, capital £50,000 (ibid., p. 51). The war ended with production more or less at a standstill.

Despite this situation there was optimism on the part of British producers, who expected to be able to revive the export of their films once hostilities had finished. In other words, a resumption of the pre-war status quo; but, of course, this ignored the progress made by Hollywood during the war years. In 1920 the *Kinematograph Year Book* expressed doubts about British producers facing the future with sufficient realism. They were also criticised for following the easy path of adaptations and focusing on cheapness.

Of the pre-war directors, Cecil Hepworth continued to operate at his studios at Walton-on-Thames and had a great post-war success with *Alf's Button* (1920). The outlook was promising, but he decided to launch a public company (proposed capital £250,000) while the trade recession was at its height and the issue flopped. The City remained wary of the film industry and subsequently Hepworth went bankrupt in 1924. George Pearson also emerged in the early twenties and in partnership with T.A. Walsh produced a number of successful films, including *Nothing Else Matters* (1920) and *Reveille* (1924). Their films were based on original screenplays and this was an important factor in their popularity. Sir Oswald Stoll entered the film business in 1918 and established studios at Richmond and then Cricklewood. At first the studios were busy, but a series of expensive failures followed, including *The Prodigal* (1923) and *The Virgin Queen* (1923).

Another figure to emerge was Graham Cutts, who made *Woman to Woman* (1923), which was the most successful British film in commercial terms before the coming of sound. And it was significant in that two of its producers were Michael Balcon and Victor Saville and the money raised for the film, around £35,000, came from C. M. Woolf, Oscar Deutsch and others – all men who were to play prominent parts in the development of the industry in the 1930s. The film was made at Islington studios, where a young Alfred Hitchcock worked in the Art Titles Department. He became assistant director on the film and wrote the script with Cutts.

Woman to Woman was well received in the US, but it was the exception and in 1926 only 26 feature films were produced in Britain. The trade was appalled and so was the government.

In 1922 the trade had been shocked to learn that of 420 films offered for sale in America only 6 had been bought. Meanwhile important overseas films such as *The Four Horsemen of the Apocalypse* (1922) were proving hugely popular with British audiences. The year 1924 was designated British Film Year with British Film Weeks being sponsored in towns throughout the country. It failed because of lack of quality and at the end of the year came 'Black November', as Charles Oakley has called it (Oakley 1964, p. 75). In that month not a single foot of negative was exposed on any studio floor in the country.

The severity of the downturn can be measured by the declining fortunes of Stoll and Ideal Films. In tandem they provided 30% of British films produced in 1921 and in 1925 Ideal made no films at all. Stoll, however, made 17 and this represented 37% of the total; the following year the company produced 5; in 1927 only 3, the year in which it was estimated that a mere 5% of the films shown in this country were British and up to 90% American (Low 1971, p. 157).

The worsening situation led to rumours of government legislation to protect the British industry. Both before and after the Quota Act, there was considerable activity as new companies were formed and old ones reorganised. The 1920s had seen the arrival of many new producers who were more keenly aware of the need for adequate capital and sound distribution deals. Michael Balcon, whose background was provincial renting, had registered Gainsborough Studios in 1924 and the group was relaunched as Gainsborough Pictures

(1928) Ltd with a capital of £262,500 in April 1928. Herbert Wilcox, who had also been involved in renting, launched British & Dominions Film Corporation as a public company in 1928 with a capital of £500,000 (ibid., p. 177). Most significantly, John Maxwell's British International Pictures was formed as a public company in 1927 with an authorised capital of £600,000 (£312,500 issued). The flotation was well timed, attracting investment before the City again grew cautious of production companies. In the same year, Maxwell arranged a merger between First National and Pathé, who combined with PCT, United Artists and Lowes Inc. to form a grouping that incorporated production, distribution and exhibition – another example of the trade's movement towards vertical integration (ibid., p. 187). BIP itself, with studios at Elstree, flourished and in its first year of operations made a profit of £200,000 (ibid., p. 190).

EXHIBITION

According to the *Kinematograph Year Book* of 1915, the number of cinemas in Britain in 1914 was around 3,500. Some estimates put the figure much higher, but Rachael Low suggests that 4,000 would have been 'the largest figure possible' (Low 1949, p. 23). The biggest circuit was Albany Ward with 29 cinemas. Ward had been a 'town hall' showman and later his circuit merged with PCT Ltd, which had 18 cinemas in 1914. The George Green circuit, based in Scotland, had 10. These were the three largest circuits at the time, but a total of 109 circuits had two or more cinemas (13% of the total). By 1920 the number of circuits under separate ownership had risen to 151, 19% of all circuit cinemas, while the circuits with ten or more cinemas had fallen to 11, 29% of circuit cinemas (PEP 1952, p. 36).

It was a period when the small independent company still predominated, but that was to change fairly rapidly as the public demanded more luxurious cinemas, and the individual theatre owner was often unable to finance the modernisation required. The 'independents' were generally undercapitalised and companies such as PCT Ltd, together with its subsidiary, APPH Ltd, prospered, and by 1920 had 68 cinemas (including those acquired when it gained control of Albany Ward). PCT Ltd had increased its nominal capital to £3.2 million and was in 1926 'the most important film company in Great Britain' with Lord Beaverbrook as one of its major shareholders (ibid., p. 35).

The exhibitors also had to contend with the introduction of the amusements tax (later known as entertainments tax) in 1916. The Chancellor of the Exchequer, Reginald McKenna, claimed that it was a temporary measure but it was not abolished until 1960. In May 1916 additional charges were introduced on cinema and theatre seats at the rate of ½d on prices up to and including 2d, rising to 1s on 12s 6d seats, plus 1s on every 10s or part of 10s after that. The revenue from this tax was expected to be around £22 million per year. The industry calculated that some 80% of this figure would come from the cheapest cinema seats.

At first the general response of the trade was muted and there was no marked fall in cinema attendances. But soon a greater appreciation of the burden placed on the small exhibitors led to protests in Parliament and hopes that the tax might be dropped. The plight of the small cinema-owner was illustrated in the *Bioscope* of 24 August 1916, which reported that a Bradford hall recorded a turnaround from a profit of £6 or £7 to a weekly loss of £5. And by 1918 the same paper reported that 700 cinemas had closed since its introduction. Despite vigorous campaigning, the tax remained in place and, apart from minor concessions regarding prices, it continued, an 'intolerable imposition' on the trade.

In addition to the restrictions imposed during the war, the small operator had to suffer rising costs, including electricity, labour and the hire of longer feature films. The average admission prices (3d, 6d and 9d) could not be increased in isolation and it was only towards the end of the war, in the wake of the amusements tax, that the Cinematograph Exhibitors' Association agreed to a general rise.

Meanwhile the larger exhibitors prospered and the movement towards circuit-building continued. It was based on sound business logic. Economies of scale could be achieved, as well as greater bargaining power with producers, and the greater bargaining power led to the hire of films at a cheaper rate. The demand for bigger, more luxurious cinemas grew and many of the new cinemas seated over 3,000 people. The image of the fleapit was receding and new films such as *The Birth of a Nation*, shown at the Scala Theatre in London in 1915, were helping to establish the cinema as an art form. Continuous performances of films around the country were becoming established and the use of publicity to boost box-office receipts was developing at this time.

The presentation of *The Birth of a Nation* as an 'exclusive' caused further trouble between the renters and the exhibitors. The battle of 'free market' versus exclusives (mainly longer films) was reaching its climax and in the end the large exhibitors, with the financial backing necessary to adjust their business methods, accepted the inevitable. The Essanay Company, who owned the Charlie Chaplin comedies, announced that all its future output would be classified as 'exclusive' and that it would be released directly to exhibitors.

During the 1920s the exhibitors prospered, attracting institutional investment once it was realised that a strong growth opportunity existed. In 1920 Lord Burnham said at a dinner of the Cinematograph Exhibitors' Association (CEA) that 'the high financiers of the world are flocking into the cinema industry' (*Bioscope*, 18 March 1920) but it was primarily the large groups and circuits that benefited. The independents struggled, either forced out of business through the refusal of renters to deal with small cooperatives, or obliged to form circuits of their own. The independents had been founded by private, often local, capital and the structure of the exhibition trade was changing to one of public companies who were themselves evolving into vertically integrated combines. By 1927 it was estimated that between £30 million and £50 million was invested in exhibition and the Blue Book listed 53 public limited liability companies with an interest in exhibition, authorised capital £11 million (Blue Book 1927–28).

The exhibitors as a whole gained some relief in 1924 when entertainments tax was removed from seats up to 6d in price and reduced on those up to 1s 3d. But efforts to remove the tax altogether failed, and meanwhile the exhibitors had to suffer the activities of American companies, specifically the practice of block and blind booking. Block booking involved a British exhibitor hiring a film from an American company on the understanding that he took a series of films. This system guaranteed the acquisition of British screen time for months ahead. More politely, it was referred to as advance booking. Blind booking worked on much the same basis, but the difference was that the exhibitor had to take the films unseen and often unmade. The exhibitor was in a cleft stick, as other films were unavailable to fill the screens, i.e. British productions, and the existence of the system deterred British film-makers. In addition, British films were more expensive to rent. An ordinary British film was said to cost £200 a week to rent in 1926, whereas an American 'super' feature cost £70 (*Bioscope*, 9 December 1926).

The Hollywood studios were providing the films that British audiences wanted to see and attendances rose accordingly. The exhibitors took the largest percentage of box-office receipts, which had reached nearly £35 million in 1927, and although the trend towards circuit-building and combination was based on sound business principles, the wish to present a united front against growing US domination also played a part in the equation.

By 1927 PCT Ltd was the largest exhibitor with 85 cinemas, followed by Moorhouse Film Service, based in Manchester with 28, Scottish Cinema & Variety Theatres with 26, Thos. Ormiston with 24, and Gaumont-British Picture Corporation with 21 (PEP 1952, p. 37). The privately owned Biocolour Picture Theatres (London) Ltd, which had been a rival of PCT Ltd in the early twenties with 25 cinemas, was sold to a syndicate backed by the Ostrer brothers in 1926 and became the basis of GBPC's growth as a circuit.

The trend towards larger companies continued and in 1927 the number of circuits owning ten or more cinemas had risen to 23, representing 13% of the cinemas in the country – the same percentage that 109 circuits had owned in 1914 (ibid., p. 36). The actual number of cinemas, according to the *Kinematograph Year Book* of 1927, was 4,075 (including Ireland) in 1920 and 4,230 in 1926 (again including Ireland). Many small cinemas closed, but others were built when building restrictions were lifted, or converted from existing theatres. The figures are a useful guide rather than hard fact since many of the 'cinemas' were possibly halls where films were shown occasionally.

DISTRIBUTION

While continuing to provide popular films for British audiences in the post-war years, the American industry began to dominate via the distribution side of the business. Given the size of their own home market, and because the costs of a particular film could often be recovered in toto, producers were able to offer their films at a cheaper rate in overseas markets and British exhibitors were happy to 'buy American'. Many of the larger companies already had offices in England by 1920 or earlier, and in that year the leading company, Famous-Lasky (Paramount) offered a total of 89 films (3 British), Jury's Imperial (MGM) 77 (11), and Fox (Twentieth Century–Fox) 67 (1), Western Import 62 (nil) and Vitagraph (Warner Brothers) 51 (nil). The total number of feature films offered for hire was 878, of which 144 were British (16%). In 1923 that fraction had fallen to 10% and in 1926 it was 5%. The 5% figure is thought to be on the high side as only 34 British films were trade-shown in that year out of a total of 749, or 4.5% (PEP 1952, pp. 40–41).

The outbreak of war had curtailed both direct open-market sales abroad and the lucrative re-export business. The exclusive renting system looked set to dominate distribution, especially when the Essanay Company decided in 1915 to offer its films on an 'exclusive' basis (they argued that many films offered for direct sale failed to cover their costs). There was opposition and the Kinematograph Renters Society, also formed in 1915, stipulated that its members show, buy or lease a fixed proportion of first-release open-market films each month (Low 1950, p. 41).

Although forced to pay high rental charges for 'exclusives', the larger exhibitors accepted the situation, albeit grudgingly, but small firms were often unable to meet the higher costs involved. The new system also brought about block booking; as early as 1916, one exhibitor had booked all his programmes for a year in advance. This was considered a by-product of the 'exclusive' which would undermine the reputation of the trade, but the practice persisted until restrictions were imposed by the 1927 Cinematograph Films Act.

In 1920 there were a large number of small independent renters (the *Kinematograph Year Book* of 1921 lists 64); among these were British companies such as Butcher's FS, Gaumont, the Stoll Film Company and Ideal. They tended to concentrate on British films but, as the decade progressed, the increasingly poor material they had to handle and the paucity of longer films continued to affect the small renters. Yet those companies specialising in American productions grew. Famous-Lasky handled 65 films in 1926, none of them British; European, Universal's British arm, distributed 55, including one British film.; Fox handled none among its 49. Even Gaumont, which was now the fourth largest distributor, only had 5 home-grown productions in its total of 48 (PEP 1952, p. 41). The overall number of distribution companies had fallen from 64 to 43 since 1920 and the 15 large firms handling 20 films or more accounted for 50% of the total – and four of the five major distributors were American. If the renters had gained control of the British film industry by 1927, then that control had its roots in Hollywood.

REGULATION

The plight of the British film industry became a matter of serious concern by the mid 1920s. British producers were clearly unable to compete with Hollywood, and the American distribution network in London had a stranglehold on the domestic market. The situation was discussed in the House of Lords in May 1925 and the peers were not unsympathetic to the industry's problems. They also accepted that the film had an important role to play in reflecting British society, i.e. propaganda, as well as being a potential dollar earner.

Negotiations began with the various branches of the trade and two sets of proposals were published. One, from the Federation of British Industries (FBI), reflected the producers' demands and suggested a quota of 12.5%, rising to 37.5% in subsequent years. This recommendation echoed a scheme first put forward in 1917 that exhibitors should show a fixed number of British films in their cinemas. The FBI also proposed the formation of a 'semi-official body' to provide loans to producers.

The second proposal, which came from a joint trade committee, included a quota for both renters and exhibitors, starting at 10% in January 1927 and increasing to 25% by June 1929. It called for the abolition of blind booking and recommended that the Board of Trade be given powers to keep the industry in British hands.

The second proposal was agreed by the council of the CEA and the KRS (Kinematograph Renters' Society), but a majority of CEA members voted against it. Many exhibitors had in fact expressed doubts about a quota system on the grounds that British films were generally so poor that box-office returns would be considerably depleted. The government had warned the trade that it would act alone if voluntary agreement could not be reached and it introduced the Cinematograph Films Bill in December 1927. The bill became law and took effect from 1 January 1928.

Apart from the first act of 1909, which concerned public safety provisions and inadvertently allowed local authorities to censor pro-grammes, government intervention had been limited to wartime measures such as the McKenna duty of 1915 on film stock and the 1916 entertainments tax. Now it was realised that the trade was unable or unwilling to put its own house in order. Government action was timely for 'by 1927, the British film industry was well on the way to extinction. It could be saved only by voluntary trade action which meant, in effect, American acquiescence, or by legis-lation (PEP 1952, p. 41).

The act stipulated that renters and exhibitors had to take a quota of British films over 3,000 feet in length. In the first year the renters' quota was 7.5% and the exhibitors' 5% (the renters' higher percent-age was to give exhibitors a greater choice of films). Both figures were to increase to 20% by 1936 and remain at that level until the act expired in 1938. Blind booking was made illegal by the requirement that all films had to be registered with the Board of Trade before they were offered for hire; and no film could be registered until it had been shown to the trade. An American distributor could not now sell a British exhibitor a batch of possibly unmade films a year ahead. Advance bookings were limited to six months ahead.

The act did succeed in bringing capital into the industry, and feature film production increased as a direct result. But, as so many had warned, it was a matter of quantity rather than quality and the reputation of British films was not enhanced, at home or abroad. The booking abuses which the exhibitors had sought to outlaw con-tinued, and the American renters were quick to establish British pro-duction subsidiaries to meet their quota requirements with scant regard for content. There had been little agreement between the various trade bodies during the negotiations and the drafting of the bill, and 'the Act was a compromise, which in the end served none of them' (Low 1971, p. 98).

THE TALKIES

The advent of sound during the late twenties was dismissed by many, including the exhibitors, as a passing craze. But the early pioneers, including the Lumière brothers, had appreciated the need for a musical accompaniment to silent films. Gramophone records were used and pianists later became commonplace in the most modest of Bijous. Full orchestras were part of the programme at the new super cinemas, but the arrival of the organist made most of them redundant.

Experiments involving the synchronisation of sound with film can be traced back to Edison in the 1890s and gramophone records had been used to link film with songs before the First World War. In 1923 the British rights to De Forest Phonofilms were acquired and the company was registered with a capital of £50,000 (Low 1971, p. 202). Over the next three years trials took place in London, resulting in a series of short films which were shown at the Capitol, Haymarket, in 1926 (ibid, p. 202). At the same time, the Vitaphone Corporation of America had been making short films with the sound on disc and their early efforts culminated in Warner Brothers' first sound feature film, *The Jazz Singer*, with Al Jolson. It was premiered in America in 1927 and shown in London a year later. Its success was instant and Warner's profit for 1928 was forecast at over £1.6 million (ibid. p. 203). The talkies had arrived, and whatever doubts were expressed by critics or the trade, the public demanded them. The industry could do nothing but comply.

CHAPTER 3

The Talkies to 1939

The 1952 PEP report on the British film industry described the years 1927 to 1930 as the 'most momentous' in the industry's history (PEP 1952, p. 45). The reasons behind this statement were the arrival of sound, the Cinematograph Films Act and the rapid development of vertically integrated combines. The report went on to call those three years 'the watershed betwecn "medieval and modern" film history'. They were the prelude to a decade when, by 1934, cinema admissions averaged 18.5 million a week and prompted A.J.P. Taylor to write 30 years later:

> Though large crowds watched Association football on Saturday afternoon and attended the *palais de danse* on Saturday evenings, they were dwarfed by the crowds who attended the cinemas every night of the week. The cinema was the essential social habit of the age, a compensation perhaps for the private boxes: doll's house at one end of the scale, cinema palace at the other. The cinema slaughtered all competitors. (Taylor 1965, p. 392)

EXHIBITION

Until 1927 the pattern had been for a number of small companies, or circuits, to dominate the exhibition business. The main exception was PCT Ltd, and in that year it had 85 cinemas. But in 1929 the company was absorbed by the rapidly growing Gaumont-British Picture Corporation Ltd. The Gaumont company had established a presence in London as early as 1898 and prospered as a producer and distributor. In the early 1920s Lt Col. Bromhead and his associates bought the rights to the Gaumont name. In 1926 the Biocolour circuit which had 17 cinemas was bought by a syndicate that included the Ostrer brothers. The following year the Gaumont British Picture Corporation Ltd was formed with a share capital of £2.5 million, backed by the Ostrers (PEP 1952, p. 46). The new company was an amalgamation of Gaumont, Ideal Films Ltd, a renter and producer, W&F Film Service Ltd, a renter, and the Biocolour circuit. Over the next twelve months Gaumont-British acquired Denham Picture Houses Ltd and General Theatre Corporation Ltd; the net result was a total of 187 cinemas (ibid., p. 46). The next significant move was the acquisition of PCT Ltd, which was achieved after a battle with ABC. In February 1929 Gaumont-British had 287 cinemas and in the same month its share capital was increased to £3.75 million (ibid., p. 48). It was now the foremost vertically integrated combine in Britain, containing the three elements of the British film trade: exhibition, distribution and production (production was undertaken at the Gaumont studios in Shepherd's Bush and the Gainsborough studios in Islington, where Michael Balcon was the managing director).

The pace of Gaumont-British's expansion may well have been due to the fact that the directors were keeping at least one eye on the activities of John Maxwell. He had been involved in exhibition since 1912 and in 1928 Associated British Cinemas was incorporated with a capital of £1 million. Maxwell had become chairman of Wardour Films Ltd in 1923 and when British International Pictures Ltd was floated in 1926 as a public company (capital also £1 million), the new group had renting interests through Wardour and production at Elstree Studios, but only 29 cinemas (ibid., p. 47). This was modest by Gaumont-British standards, but Maxwell also moved quickly and in 1929 ABC had 88 cinemas and its capital was doubled to £2 million (Low 1971, p. 43). In 1933 Associated British Picture Corporation Ltd (ABPC) was formed as a holding company – Pathé Pictures Ltd had been added to the group – and the ABC circuit had grown to 147 cinemas (PEP 1952, p. 48).

While Gaumont-British and ABC remained the two leading circuits, the 1930s witnessed the emergence of a strong rival, the Odeon chain. In 1933 Cinema Service, a small circuit which owned 26 cinemas, changed its name to Odeon Pictures Ltd. It was registered as a private company with a capital of £100. Odeon's founder was Oscar Deutsch;

he was a Midlands industrialist and he became involved in the film business via distribution. Deutsch believed in building cinemas and he devised a novel way of financing part of their cost. Each new Odeon was a separate company and once its location was established, often in new towns or expanding suburbs, the capital for the purchase of the land was obtained from local business interests via the issue of preference shares. For example, the Odeon (Bognor) Ltd was launched with an authorised capital of £10,100 in 10,000 8% cumulative preference shares of £1 each, and 2,000 ordinary shares of 1s each (ibid., p. 57). The costs of building the cinema and equipping it were met by loans and mortgages from financial institutions, mainly insurance companies. Deutsch retained control by holding the majority of the ordinary shares that were issued.

Deutsch's plan was well timed. Cinema construction had been boosted by the lifting of building regulations in the 1920s, and in 1933 Simon Rowson addressed the British Kinematograph Society on the subject. His paper gave details of building costs per seat: the average for an ordinary cinema was £15 and a new, 'super' cinema around £50. The latter's total cost on the basis of 1,500 seats was estimated at between £40,000 and £70,000 (excluding the cost of the site and equipment).

Deutsch's concept of 'brand selling' worked well; the Odeons, incorporating aspects of art deco, were distinctive and popular. But he did face one problem – getting enough quality, first-run films to fill his cinemas. Gaumont-British and ABPC owned 559 cinemas between them in 1935 and they were also major producers and distributors; they were unlikely to help a formidable rival (in 1936 Odeon had grown to 142 cinemas). In the event, help came from another quarter. United Artists (UA), the American renter, had been looking for a British circuit to buy, or buy into, and in 1936 UA acquired 50% of Odeon's ordinary shares and one-third of the preference shares. They put three directors on the board, but Deutsch retained control through his casting vote at board meetings.

UA probably benefited most from the deal, but Deutsch gained from a flow of American films to put on his screens and the group's expansion continued with the acquisition of County Cinemas in 1937, bringing the total up to 250. In the same year, the Odeons were organised into a new £6 million company, Odeon Theatres, which was successfully floated on the London stock market. The prospectus emphasised that the company would not be involved in film production, and this was thought to be one of the main reasons for the success of the issue.

As the Odeon chain grew, Gaumont-British and ABPC increased the size of their circuits. In 1935 they accounted for 13% of the cinemas in the country. The following year the combined total of their cinemas had risen to 601 and the view within the industry was that Gaumont-British could become the target of American interest. In fact, control of the company lay with the Metropolis & Bradford Trust Co., which held 2.915 million ordinary shares out of the £5 million issued. Of this holding, 2.1 million shares were held on behalf of Twentieth Century–Fox (ibid., p. 66). Rumours circulated that MGM would buy a 50% stake in Fox's interest in Metropolis & Bradford.

No such deal materialised but, perhaps surprisingly, the Ostrer brothers sold John Maxwell 250,000 non-voting shares in Metropolis & Bradford together with a five-year option on Isidore Ostrer's 5,100 voting shares. The purchases were said to have cost Maxwell nearly £1.5 million (Low 1985, p. 242). Twentieth Century–Fox not unnaturally objected to a deal and vetoed the transaction. Despite this setback, ABPC continued to grow and in 1937 announced gross profits of £1.266 million and total assets of £14.750 million (ibid., p. 231). In the same year the company acquired the Union circuit bringing the total number of cinemas to around 450. ABPC was now the largest exhibitor in Britain.

The exhibitors, despite some initial doubts, came to appreciate that 'talkies' meant bigger audiences and embraced the phenomenon. What they didn't like, of course, were the costs involved in converting their cinemas to sound. These have been estimated at between £2,000 and £4,000 for the equipment alone (PEP 1952, p. 54). Many cinemas closed, unable to pass on the costs through higher admission prices. The trade as a whole still believed that the cinema provided entertainment for the masses and a rise in prices was considered unwise, both economically and socially.

The exhibitors also had to pay more for the hire of sound films. The renting companies now demanded a percentage of the box-office takings, as well as a flat rental charge for a film. After entertainments tax was deducted, the takings were split between the renter and the exhibitor, with the former sometimes taking as much as 50% from the small independent circuits. The trade bodies were unhelpful; the Kinematograph Film Makers' Association (KMA) was, in effect, controlled by American interests and the Cinematograph Exhibitors' Association (CEA) was again divided. Despite strong opposition, the system became established by the early 1930s. But some large circuits, such as Gaumont-British and ABPC, were able to negotiate from a position of financial strength and persuade the renters to accept around 20% or 25% (Low 1985, p. 3) of box-office receipts.

In 1935 Simon Rowson produced the first authoritative statistical survey of the number, size and distribution of the cinemas in Britain and their takings (ibid., p. 2). Rowson was a statistician who had founded Ideal Films Ltd, and he became a director of Gaumont-British in the 1927 amalgamation. His paper was based on 2,000 cinemas (around 43% of the total). The figures included the number of admissions to cinemas in 1934 − 963 million (an average of 18.5 million a week) − with £41.12 million taken at the box office (£6.8 million went on entertainments tax). He found that the vast majority of tickets sold were for the cheaper seats: 80% a shilling or less; 43% 6d or less. Rowson's study underlined the fact that the cinema was very much the 'working man's theatre'.

J. ARTHUR RANK

The early 1930s witnessed the arrival of the man who was to become the major figure within the British industry, J. Arthur Rank. Within ten years he would control the Gaumont-British and Odeon circuits, film studios at Pinewood, Denham, Shepherd's Bush and Elstree, and a major distribution business, General Film Distributors Ltd.

Rank's wealth was based on the family flour milling business and he was a devout Methodist. His interest in the cinema came from a belief that simple films, dealing with religious matters, could be made and shown in mission halls and schools throughout the country. As Michael Wakelin has pointed out, 'he merely wanted to promote Christianity through good films' (Wakelin 1996, p. 47). The first film he backed, *Mastership* (1934), cost £2,700 and lasted twenty minutes. More productions followed and Rank set up a company, Religious Films Ltd, to handle distribution through the network of churches and schools that had been built up, mainly by Rank himself.

During this time, Rank's interest in the commercial cinema was growing and in 1934 he formed a £6,000 private company, British National Films, in partnership with Lady Yule, the widow of a jute millionaire, and John Corfield, a producer. Rank's business sense was acute and he realised that 'overtly evangelistic films' would not be shown by the big exhibitors. Consequently, the first British National production, *The Turn of the Tide* (1935), was a story of family conflict in a North Yorkshire fishing village. It was warmly received by the critics but the distributors, Gaumont-British, virtually ignored the film. It had cost £30,000 and made only £18,000 at the box office. This confirmed Rank's low opinion of the distribution business and strengthened the logic of backing C.M. Woolf's General Film Distributors Ltd (GFD) earlier in the year. Woolf had formerly been joint managing director of Gaumont-British, and GFD was registered with 'the large capital of £270,000' (Low 1985, p. 209). He became Rank's mentor 'and was credited with guiding him through the dark vale of Wardour Street, the street where there were rumoured to be "shadows on both sides"' (Macnab 1993, p. 22).

In May 1935 Rank, in partnership with Lady Yule and Sir Charles Boot, bought Heatherden Hall in Buckinghamshire; it became Pinewood Studios at a cost of over £1 million and had 72,490 square feet of floor space on five stages. It took nine months to build and production began in September 1936 (ibid., p. 24). Pinewood Studios Ltd had been registered as a private company (£150,000 capital) and as well as Rank and Boot, the board included all the directors of British & Dominions Film Corporation (B&D) and a director of British National Films Ltd. B&D was a production company whose films were distributed by United Artists (PEP 1952, p. 61). The studios were the basis of Rank's output in the mid 1930s. In 1939 he acquired his next studios when Denham & Pinewood Ltd (D&P) was formed with a capital of £750,000 (ibid., p. 65). Korda's backers at Denham, the Prudential Assurance Company, had become increasingly concerned about the financial position of the studios and readily agreed to a reorganisation that effectively gave Rank control. Later in the year, Rank again moved swiftly, buying Amalgamated Studios at Elstree.

In March 1936 Rank had registered the General Cinema Finance Corporation (GCFC) with an authorised capital of £1.225 million. The new corporation immediately bought 90% of General Film Distributors Ltd, where Woolf remained on the board as well as being managing director of B&D. At the same time, the American company Universal was bought by a group of American and British investors that included Rank and L.W. Farrow, another GCFC director. Both had seats on the new trustee board. As a result of their participation, Universal's renting subsidiary in Britain merged with GFD, and the distribution arrangement was reciprocal (ibid., p. 62). GCFC now had major production and renting businesses, plus a small circuit of cinemas, but to complete its vertical integration a large chain was needed. This did not happen until 1941.

DISTRIBUTION

In 1926 the six leading American distributors handled only two British films between them. The 1927 Films Act stated that distributors had to take a quota of 7.5% British films during the first year of its operation, which began on 1 April 1928. The act stimulated the creation of new companies and it was possible that there would be enough films available to meet the 7.5% target. But the American distributors began to worry about the effect on their own product. Gradually, they began to sponsor British films which were cheaply made, fulfilled their quota requirements and provided no competition for their Hollywood masters. By the end of 1931, US financing of 'quota quickies' was well under way (PEP 1952, p. 51).

The American renters also began to consider the possibilities of circuit ownership in the wake of the Films Act and the growth of the two main combines. By 1929 both Gaumont-British and the Maxwell Group (as it then was) were number one and number two respectively among the distributors, offering 102 and 87 feature films for hire (18 and 15 British). Nevertheless, out of the ten leading distributors at the time, six were American companies (ibid., p. 52). The distribution business would remain the basis of their domination, but as early as

1928 Twentieth Century—Fox signalled future policy towards exhibition through its stake in the company that controlled Gaumont-British. As we have seen, United Artists became involved with Odeon in the 1930s, and Paramount had a small circuit of super cinemas.

By the mid 1930s, despite the importance of Gaumont-British Distributors (G-B) and Wardour-Pathé (ABPC's distribution arm), the American renters hired out 60% of all films marketed in Britain. G-B and Wardour handled between 20 and 30 British films a year and virtually the same number of foreign ones, some 16% of the total. Other British renters included General Film Distributors and British Lion Film Corporation with 10 or more films (ibid., p. 60).

In 1939 US dominance had been sustained: the six 'majors' still distributed over half of all feature films and another, Universal, had its films handled by GFD, now the foremost British renter, offering over 60 films a year. British Lion had dealt with Republic's films since 1935 and ABPC's distribution network was still prominent among the leading renters of the time, but Gaumont-British Distributors had ceased trading in 1937. The 1930s had seen the establishment of a pattern whereby 'distributors dominated British films, manipulating the purse-strings at will' (Macnab 1993, p. 22).

PRODUCTION

The 1927 act had an immediate effect on British film production. It became an attractive investment opportunity and there was finance around. British International Pictures Ltd (BIP) was formed in the same year and in 1928 both B&D and Gainsborough were launched. Together with London Film Productions and Ealing Studios, these companies were to become the major British producers of the 1930s. The number of new companies grew rapidly, from 26 in 1927 to 37 in 1928 and 59 in 1929 (PEP 1952, p. 22). Between 1930 and 1935 a total of 395 companies were registered, 108 in 1935 alone. As a result, British feature films rose from 96 (15.7% of all features) in the year to 31 March 1930 to 215 (29.5%) in the year to 31 March 1936 (ibid., p. 60). The volume of British features far exceeded both the renters' and the exhibitors' quotas over the period.

In 1928 the first British sound films were registered and the first commercially successful British talkie was Alfred Hitchcock's *Blackmail*, which was trade-shown in June 1929. John Maxwell's BIP had produced the film and soon other studios such as Gainsborough and Ealing had converted to sound film production. The availability of capital eased the transition and it also enabled studios to expand, e.g. Gaumont-British at Shepherd's Bush. Older studios at Cricklewood, Twickenham and Beaconsfield were revived. Unfortunately, their revival often meant a production programme of quota quickies.

The BIP studios were busy in the first half of the 1930s, with further films from Hitchcock, musicals and Will Hay comedies. BIP's profits fell to £110,426 in the financial year 1932–33 and ABC's profits halved to £105,261 (Low 1985, p. 122) in the same period, largely due to the effects of the Depression. Maxwell responded by amalgamating the two companies into ABPC and by 1936 the new group was making gross profits of £926,042 (ibid., p. 123). By then BIP had cut back on film production, a decision influenced by the lack of an American market for its output, and although it had picked up again by 1938, one suspects that Maxwell's real interest lay in circuit-building. But during the decade over 200 films had been made at Elstree.

In the early 1930s Gaumont-British gained control of Gainsborough Studios and Michael Balcon became head of production at both Islington and Shepherd's Bush. There were initial successes: *Rome Express* (1932), *The Good Companions* (1933) and *I Was a Spy* (1933). However, film production was not profitable, yet following a reorganisation at Gaumont-British in 1933 (the share capital was increased to £6.25 million and a new £5 million debenture stock was issued), output was expanded. During the next few years there were George Formby and Will Hay comedies, some of the best prewar Alfred Hitchcock thrillers – *The Man Who Knew Too Much* (1934) and *The Thirty-Nine Steps* (1935) – and more Jessie Matthews musicals. The average cost of Gainsborough and Gaumont films was not excessive: £30,000 to £40,000 for an average feature, around £50,000 to £70,000 for a musical (ibid., p. 142). Although film production made a small profit of £12,000 in 1935, the following year recorded losses of £97,000 (ibid., p. 143). Again, the lack of American distribution was at the heart of the problem. When Isidore Ostrer, the president of Gaumont-British, returned from the United States in January 1937, he outlined the seriousness of the position:

> Unless we can get a bigger American revenue, we must discontinue the production of big pictures for the international market. The whole situation was reviewed by me when I was in the United States and will be discussed by the Gaumont-British Board, and I expect that the possibilities will be so far clarified that we shall be able to make a decision by the end of March.
>
> Producers, over a period of time, cannot avoid loss on production, unless substantial revenue is received from all the important English-speaking countries. American producers can only produce at a loss unless they receive a substantial revenue from Britain, and British producers cannot effectively carry on without receiving a substantial net revenue from America.
>
> American film companies are receiving big revenues from England – in the aggregate probably between £7,000,000 and £10,000,000 net per year, but British producers receive a negligible amount from America, probably not more than £200,000 a year. (*Financial Times*, 21 January 1937)

In the event, Shepherd's Bush studios were closed, with limited production continuing at Islington. Balcon had left at the end of 1936 and there was an emphasis on comedy films after his departure. Of greater significance to the industry was the announcement in 1937 that it was no longer an economic proposition to keep Gaumont-British Distributors in full operation.

British & Dominions Film Corporation was a £500,000 company with a studio adjacent to BIP at Elstree and, perhaps more importantly, it had a distribution deal with Gaumont-British. The studio was converted to sound and Herbert Wilcox's first films included adaptations of Aldwych farces and a series of pictures with Jack Buchanan and Anna Neagle. They were commercially successful and at first B&D was profitable; but the company was undercapitalised and by 1935 loss-making. The previous year an attempt at reconstruction had failed, but in 1936 a fire destroyed the B&D studios. Wilcox entered into an arrangement with Rank at Pinewood Studios which gave B&D a stake in the new company. He went on to make *Victoria the Great* in 1937; it proved a huge success and it was distributed in the United States by RKO, a major breakthrough for British productions. *Sixty Glorious Years* (1938) was also commercially successful. In that year a partnership deal was struck with RKO-Radio to produce three or four films a year, but by 1939 Wilcox and his production companies had gone bankrupt.

There had been film studios at Ealing since 1907, but in 1931 Basil Dean's Associated Talking Pictures, which was floated in 1929 with a capital of £125,000, built new studios to the south of the old premises. It was fully equipped for sound production and much of the equipment was provided by RKO, with whom the company had a distribution deal. The actual cost far exceeded the original estimate of £70,000, but the studios were completed. Demand for new films was great and 'in the next seven years, some 60 feature films were made at Ealing. Half of them were made by Dean's company, ATP, the rest by other companies who simply rented space' (Barr 1977, p. 4). A series of films with Gracie Fields established the studio after a shaky start and the George Formby comedies which followed were also very popular. But the company was losing money; in 1937 it lost £97,679 and the following year £35,443 (Low 1985, p. 252). In 1938 Dean left, blamed for the decline, and after a brief period with MGM, Michael Balcon took over as head of production. The name of the company was changed from ATP to Ealing Studios Ltd.

The most important company to emerge in the early thirties was Alexander Korda's London Film Productions, formed in 1931. By 1933 Korda had produced five Paramount-British quota films and in that year he made *The Private Life of Henry VIII* for London Films. United Artists put money into the film and took on distribution. It cost around £60,000 to make, it was immensely popular in the United States, and before it had completed its first world run it was said to have made £500,000 (ibid., p. 168). The film was seen as a blueprint for international success and institutional investors, who had been wary of backing films in the previous year or two, reappeared, including Lloyd's of London.

In 1934 London Films' share capital was increased to £825,000, the bulk of which came from Prudential Assurance and other City institutions and banks. It was Korda's *annus mirabilis* with box-office hits like *Catherine the Great* and *The Scarlet Pimpernel*. The films were lavish and consequently expensive, but they were immensely popular at home and abroad. The Korda philosophy appeared to be working. In 1935, though, there was only one real hit, *The Ghost Goes West*, and by this time Korda was involved in the construction of Denham Studios at a cost of £1 million plus. Opened in May 1936, they were the biggest studios in England, used for London Films' productions and by outside producers. The lack of profitable films led to losses of £330,842 in 1936 but 1937 saw a turnaround to profits of £35,839 (ibid., p. 221). The Prudential was becoming concerned as the number of independent producers at Denham declined, and as the major shareholder and chief creditor sought to put the company on a more stable financial footing. The outcome was a merger of Denham and Pinewood in 1939; this gave control to Rank while Korda embarked on an independent career with Alexander Korda Productions.

Korda's impact on the British cinema and its finances was considerable. For a brief period in the mid 1930s he seemed to have the 'magic touch' and City institutions were eager to fund a film-maker who could guarantee international success. When the slump came, he was a convenient scapegoat, cited as an example of the financial extravagance that had contributed to the industry's downfall. What his critics failed to recognise, or simply ignored, was that the expansion of British production had been based on very shaky foundations. Korda alone could not be held responsible for the collapse.

QUOTA QUICKIES

American companies made arrangements to produce films in Britain to fulfil their quotas. Warner Brothers and Twentieth Century–Fox already had subsidiaries in this country and the other US majors used British producers to make their quota quickies. There was little interest in the quality of these films and this had a devastating effect on the reputation of the British industry. George Pearson recalled their production:

> The usual budget for a 'quickie' was determined solely on length, based on a fixed charge of £1 per foot of screened film – hence

the 'quickies' were sarcastically termed 'Pound-a-Footers'. Their average length was between five and six thousand feet, enough for an hour of screen time sufficient for the Quota. To make a talking film with £6,000 only to meet the costs of studio space, subject, script, director, technicians, film stock, lights, artistes, overheads, and end up with a profit, needed a Spartan economy and a slave-driving effort, for the time allotted on the floor was strictly limited to twelve days, less if possible! (Pearson 1957, pp. 192–93)

He went on to describe the mechanics of production:

'Quota 'quickie' making followed a rigid formula: first an agreement on some inexpensive subject, some story selected from the scores of such submitted by would-be authors, since the cost of the film-rights of a published novel would swamp the budget, followed by a fortnight's team work by the film-director and a dialogue writer usually attached to the studio staff. Oh, those dialogue discussions! Given the narrative sequence of scenes with their content described in detail, the dialogue inventor could set to work, stop watch in hand. His contribution to each scene became the arbiter of its time length. When all was finished, it might be found that the total length was too long or too short by seconds or even minutes. If too long, the axe went to work, for elimination was always profitable pruning. (ibid., p. 193)

Unfortunately, his own company, Welsh-Pearson, went into liquidation in the early thirties, but with the help of Michael Balcon he managed to stay in the industry.

The determination with which Hollywood adapted to the new circumstances can be illustrated by the fact that 'in 1931 the seven major American distributors had their 44 quota films supplied by 36 different British producers' (Street 1997, p. 9). Production was expanding but not in the way that the government had intended. Nevertheless, the statutory minima for both the renters and exhibitors were exceeded by considerable margins during the first half of the 1930s. In 1934–35, for example, the exhibitors' quota was 20% but the actual figure was 27.4%. British films were clearly being shown in cinemas but their quality was generally poor, and quota quickies continued to be made until the new Cinematograph Films Act of 1938.

THE SLUMP

During the 1930s money poured into the production companies. Between 1928 and 1938 studio space increased from 105,200 square feet to 777,650 square feet and the value of production in 1937 was put at £7 million, up from £500,000 in 1928 (PEP 1952, p. 67). In the year to 31 March 1938, 228 British films were registered. The outward signs were of a prosperous industry, but this was not the case:

> It was *World Film News*, however, that blew the gaff. In an article published at the beginning of 1937, much discussed in the City (and later published as a brochure), it said: 'banks, insurance companies, investment trusts, even motor manu-facturers have been falling over each other in their eagerness to join in the Gold Rush and to stake a claim. Yet, in spite of the torrent of money in which British production companies have revelled, few have paid a dividend since 1932 ... and, as most of them have been formed since 1932, that means most have never paid a dividend at all.' (Oakley 1964, p. 134)

The article went on to suggest that the Official Receiver would be the star of a lavish new production about to be filmed.

In the same month, January 1937, receivers were appointed at Julius Hagen's Twickenham studios and pay cuts implemented at London Films. There was also a rumour on the stock market that Gaumont-British would defer payment of the dividend on its 5.5% preference shares (*Financial Times*, 15 January 1937). The rumour was untrue, but indicated growing unease in the City. Later in the year, the Gainsborough losses were announced and Shepherd's Bush studios closed.

April 1937 was the month in which a group of Lloyd's under-writers set up a committee to investigate film production in general and the activities of Aldgate Trustees Ltd in particular. The man behind Aldgate was Max Schach and in 1934 he formed Capitol Film

Productions. His plan was that each film would be financed individually. His method involved the acquisition of a guarantee on the production from a Lloyd's underwriter, via a firm of insurance brokers. The guarantee would then be presented at a bank and the money borrowed against it. His first film, *Abdul the Damned* (1934), was a co-production with BIP and Schach's share of the cost was £15,000, borrowed from the Westminster Bank (Low 1985, p. 199).

The film's success led in 1935 to the creation of Aldgate Trustees Ltd, a private trustee company. Schach registered a larger company, Capitol Film Corporation (capital £125,000), and other new companies such as British Cine Alliance, Cecil Films, Trafalgar Film Productions, City Film Corporation and Buckingham Film Productions all benefited from Aldgate money, raised from banks on Lloyd's guarantees.

Few films, if any, were being made by these companies and the trade became alarmed during 1936. In 1937 *World Film News* published details of the charges on the Schach companies to the Aldgate trustees: Capitol owed £1.1 million, Trafalgar £450,000 and Cecil and Buckingham £150,000 each; and there were others. Between January and October 1936 production companies borrowed in excess of £4,050,000 (Klingender and Legg 1937, p. 48), of which 65% went to Schach companies.

The publication of these statistics and the results of the underwriters' investigations effectively ended the production boom. They also led to legal action by the Westminster Bank against 15 insurance companies for losses on production; the insurance companies brought a counter-claim. The case was heard in May 1939 and settled out of court after six days. Both parties had shown surprising naivety in failing to insist on proper accounting methods and controls on spending within the companies concerned, especially Capitol. By this time production had declined dramatically – in the year to 31 March 1939 only 103 British films were registered – and the case provided a sour epilogue to British film financing in the 1930s.

By the end of 1937 the boom was over. British producers had been faced with the choice of either making inexpensive quota films or attempting to gain a foothold in world markets with expensive, Hollywood-style, productions. The success of *Henry VIII* suggested it was possible to achieve international glory and this led to over-investment in the following years, mainly by insurance brokers and others with little experience of the film business. The assumption that British films would find an overseas market was illusory, especially when the Americans had ignored the reciprocity agreement made after the 1927 act: 'one British film would be released in the United States for every 15 or 20 American films released in Great Britain' (Oakley 1964, p. 135). And to compete with Hollywood, the home-grown product had to be more expensive, even extravagant, as many claimed. Costs escalated and proved a contributory factor in the demise of many companies. News of bankruptcies and studio closures came at a time when film-makers were cutting back on production ahead of the 1938 Films Act; uncertainty regarding the quota arrangements was the principal reason.

The expansion in the 1930s was based on false confidence, and the 1937 collapse made investors even more cautious of the business. As a result of the activities of the Aldgate trustees, among others, 'film finance was indeed "brought into disrepute"' (PEP 1952, p. 73).

REGULATION

Against this background, the government introduced the Cinematograph Films Act of 1938. In 1936 the Moyne Committee was set up by the government to 'consider the position of British films', mainly in the context of the approaching demise of the 1927 act. The committee concluded that the quota system would be retained and extended; the earlier act had failed to check US domination of the home market and some form of protectionism was considered desirable. They also recommended that quotas should apply to long and short films and that there should be a quality test to avoid the worst aspects of the 'quota quickie' and that this test would be administered by a Films Commission. The setting up of a body to 'finance British film production', under the government, was suggested.

As before, the trade bodies were deadlocked on the proposals and the government went ahead independently. Quotas were accepted as necessary and were applied to long and short films. The 'long' quota was reduced to 15% for renters and 12.5% for exhibitors during the first year, subsequently rising to 30% and 25% in the final year, 1946. The act did not introduce a quality test (and it did not accept the idea of a Films Commission: an advisory body continued under the new title of the Cinematograph Films Council) and relied instead on a cost calculation: if labour costs on any given film were less than £7,500 then that film would not qualify for the quota. The trade thought this figure was inadequate. Blind and advance booking remained illegal. On the broader front of film finance coming under a government-supported, or government-encouraged, body there was silence.

The act also introduced a system of double and treble quotas. Films with labour costs of £3 per foot and a minimum length of 7,500 feet counted as twice that length and films at £5 per foot (and 7,500 feet in length) counted as three times that length for the renters' quota (PEP 1952, p. 77). The aim was to encourage more first feature films.

The immediate result of the act was to galvanise US companies into production in Britain. MGM, Twentieth Century–Fox and Warner Brothers announced programmes of films that would be made in studios such as Pinewood and the reconstructed Teddington. Meanwhile the British combines continued to build their circuits as the act failed to tempt them back into serious production.

There were misgivings about the effectiveness of the 1938 act. In its first year, British output fell to 103 films; by early 1939 production was valued at £4.5 million, against £5.7 million (Low 1985, p. 52), and employment in production had nearly halved since the slump began. Many studios were empty or closed. Some blamed the City scandals and uncertainty ahead of the act for the downturn. Whatever the reasons, British producers still faced their perennial problem – the lack of a world market for their films. But it was a problem that would shrink in significance as September 1939 approached.

CHAPTER 4

The Second World War: 1939–45

The immediate response of the government to the outbreak of war in September 1939 was to close cinemas across the country. The risk of bombing by enemy aircraft was the reason behind the decision, but the measure was short-lived. The harmful effect on the nation's morale was emphasised by trade bodies within the industry; also the economic aspects were stressed: a loss of £200,000 a week in taxation and 75,000 jobs at risk (Oakley 1964, p. 152). The cinemas reopened and audiences grew considerably during the course of the war years: in 1939 weekly attendances averaged 19 million, by 1945 they had reached 30 million (ibid., p. 152).

EXHIBITION

In 1939 the three main circuits – Gaumont-British, ABPC and Odeon – owned over 1,000 cinemas between them, 21% of the total, and there were 14 circuits with over 20 cinemas, 30% of the total (PEP 1952, p. 80). American interest was limited to the stakes held by United Artists in Odeon and Twentieth Century–Fox in Gaumont-British, plus some pre-release cinemas in London.

Once the period of closure passed, the cinema owners had to face the likely impact of the war on their business. No new cinemas could be built – a blessing in disguise according to many in the industry – and the call-up of staff plus actual bomb damage meant that many cinemas did close (around 10% is the estimate). In 1939 there had been approximately 4,800 cinemas in Britain and, according to Board of Trade statistics, this figure had fallen to 4,415 by the end of 1941. However, in the Palache Committee Report of July 1944 it was estimated that there were 4,750 cinemas in Great Britain and Northern Ireland. The three major circuits controlled 1,061 cinemas (ABPC 442, Gaumont-British 304 and Odeon 315), of which 966 were open. Their seating capacity was put at around 1,500,000, one-third of the total. Average weekly attendances were 'in excess' of 25 million (*Financial Times*, 2 August 1944).

The primary difficulty facing exhibitors was the supply of new films. According to the trade, some 600 films were needed annually to fill British screens. The Treasury, anxious to curb dollar expenditure, fixed the number of American films at 400. In 1939 a total of 638 feature films were registered in Great Britain (535 were 'foreign'); by 1941 this figure had fallen to 465 (400). Old films were reissued and extended runs introduced. Despite the lower number of new films, attendances continued to grow and over the course of the war box-office takings trebled (PEP 1952, pp. 82–83).

The government also imposed limits on remittances paid to American producers by means of the 1939 Anglo-American Film Agreement. In that year £7 million had been remitted; in the following three years amounts of £4.8 million, £5.7 million and £8.5 million were transferred (ibid., p. 98). During this period there was a reciprocal arrangement whereby quota obligations were eased for US companies using 'blocked' earnings to make films in Britain. Gradually the restrictions were relaxed, especially after the United States entered the war in December 1941, and in the year ending 31 October 1943 £26.5 million was paid, representing current earnings plus the release of £12 million in 'blocked' funds (ibid., p. 98). Thereafter the restrictions were abandoned.

The wartime boom in attendances boosted the Treasury's coffers via three increases in entertainments tax. In 1939 this stood at approximately 16% of gross receipts; by 1945 it was closer to 36% (ibid., p. 83). The Palache Committee cited the 1943–44 financial year:

> According to a reply given on 2nd May 1944, by the Financial Secretary to the Treasury to a question in the House of Commons, entertainments tax receipts from cinemas amounted in the

financial year 1943–44 to £37,277,000. The average percentage of the gross admission price which is paid in tax under the rates applicable as from 16th May 1943, is not known to us, states the committee, but it would not appear unreasonable to assume it to be about 33⅓ per cent. This would give a total box office receipt figure of £112,000,000 or, say, £110 millions for the year; that is, £70–75 millions net receipts after payment of tax. (*Financial Times*, 2 August 1944)

As well as the burden of entertainments tax, the exhibitors were also faced with a potential liability to excess profits tax as audiences and box-office takings grew. They certainly benefited from the boom, but not to the extent that they would have wished.

DISTRIBUTION

The distribution business changed little during the war. In 1939 the six leading US combines distributed over 50% of all feature films (PEP 1952, p. 79) and the medium-sized renter United Artists was influential through its stake in the Odeon chain. Universal's films were distributed through Rank's General Film Distributors (GFD), the most important British company, which handled about 60 films per year. Also prominent were British Lion, who distributed Republic's films, and ABPC's distribution arm. Associated British Film Distributors, part-owners of Ealing Studios, handled some 20 films a year. In 1945 the overall position was much the same.

PRODUCTION

In 1939 British film production was still suffering from the effects of the 1937 crash and only 103 feature films were released in that year. The major production companies were Rank's General Cinema Finance Corporation (GCFC) with Denham, Pinewood and Amalgamated Studios linked to the most important British distributor, GFD; ABPC, with studios at Welwyn and Elstree; and Gaumont-British, with its studios at Shepherd's Bush and Islington (also distributing its films through GFD). These groups controlled about 50% of the studio space. Four American companies, Twentieth Century–Fox, MGM, Paramount and Warner Brothers – with studios at Teddington – had established production facilities in Britain by 1939 (Oakley 1964, p. 153).

As war broke out, Pinewood and Amalgamated were operating at well below capacity and, subsequently, these studios plus Elstree and Sound City were requisitioned by the government. As a result, around half the studio space in Britain was under government control and was used primarily for the making of propaganda films by the Ministry of Information or for storage purposes. (Rank was apparently quite happy with the requisition: there were no new productions in hand to occupy the floor space and he received an income from the government at a time when the studios might have been idle.)

Although the number of feature films registered in the year to 31 March 1940 increased marginally to 108, the following year saw a sharp decline to 45. In 1942 the figure was 46, in 1943 it was 62, in 1944 it was 70 and in 1945 it was 67 (statistics from the Board of Trade). Given fears that British production might be abandoned completely, and the difficult conditions that prevailed, including major shortages of labour and equipment, an average of around 60 films a year was quite respectable; but there was criticism of the producers on the grounds of lack of planning and an undue emphasis on expensive films. However, it was argued that more lavish productions provided an opportunity to break into the lucrative American market. There was some basis to the argument. Since the United States entered the war in 1941, Hollywood output had waned and there was at least a glimmer of business logic in the attempt to win US audiences with ambitious films. But they were more expensive to make, and it was pointed out that 'a first feature made in 1940 for £42,000 would have cost three times as much had it been produced in 1944' (PEP 1952, p. 84).

The success of *In Which We Serve* (1942) and *49th Parallel* (1942) convinced many, including Rank, that British production should be aimed at the international market. At the same time, a new kind of British cinema was developing, one that mirrored the everyday lives of people at war. Many films were made that reflected national character, such as *The Way Ahead* (1944) and *The Way to the Stars* (1945), which succeeded as propaganda and works of art. Some were influenced by the British documentary tradition (notable itself for wartime films) and as the war drew to a close, the British film was enjoying a renaissance that was appreciated both at home and overseas. It had been achieved during a period when the industry had only 9 of its 22 studios in use and around 30% of its pre-war technicians.

CONSOLIDATION

'Whereas the rest of the industry had been contracting since the beginning of the war, Rank had been expanding' (Macnab 1993, p. 42). The emergence of J. Arthur Rank was discussed in Chapter 3. The consolidation of his position began in 1941 when he bought a controlling interest in both Gaumont-British Picture Corporation and Odeon Theatres Ltd.

The year before John Maxwell had died. At the time of his death he held an option on 5,100 voting shares in Metropolis & Bradford Trust, the company that controlled Gaumont-British. The board of ABPC allowed the option to lapse and Rank stepped in, buying the shares from the Ostrer brothers for around £750,000 in October 1941. The share purchase represented 51% of the voting capital; the remaining 49% was held by Twentieth Century–Fox, who did not object to the acquisition. Perhaps ironically, in August 1941 Warner Brothers, through its British subsidiary, had bought a 25% stake in ABPC for just over £900,000 (*Financial Times*, 23 February 1946).

Rank had become interested in Odeon Theatres Ltd in 1938 when he made a modest investment in the company. He joined the board in 1939 and when Oscar Deutsch died suddenly in December 1941 Rank acquired Odeon via a network of holding companies. He had purchased a very successful circuit – 1941 saw record profits of £1.5 million (Macnab 1993, p. 29) – and it was a development that Deutsch would have endorsed as it saved Odeon from falling into American hands.

Rank's empire now consisted of exhibition (619 cinemas, Odeon and Gaumont-British combined), distribution (General Film Distributors Ltd, on a par with the leading US renters) and production (Pinewood, Denham and Amalgamated Studios). There were other subsidiary businesses, including film equipment and radio manufacturing, but the core activities – exhibition, distribution and production – represented the most successful example of vertical integration in the history of the British film industry.

Following his acquisition of Gaumont-British, Rank began a production drive and during the war years Gainsborough Studios made 22 features costing £1.3 million and grossing £2.6 million (ibid., p. 115). Their melodramas such as *The Man in Grey* (1943) were very successful and continued to be popular in the post-war era. At Denham, Del Guidice's Two Cities company had a string of hits beginning with *In Which We Serve* (1942). Later productions included *This Happy Breed* (1944), *Henry V* (1944) and *The Way to the Stars* (1945). Their patriotic nature appealed to audiences at the time, and many of the films have since been acknowledged as British classics.

Rank also set up Independent Producers Ltd at Denham, which included a disparate collection of production teams, such as the Archers, Cineguild and Wessex. They were given freedom and finance. In 1944 Ealing Studios came under Rank's wing with a distribution deal and the provision of up to 75% of production costs.

Rank's conviction that British films should be sold internationally led to the creation of Eagle-Lion Distributors Ltd in 1944. A network of offices was established throughout the world to promote British films. The structure was in place; all that was needed was a steady supply of pictures that overseas audiences wanted to see.

INTERVENTION

In spite of the restrictions imposed by a wartime economy, the major combines, especially the Rank group, increased their domination of the domestic film industry. In the sphere of production, the continuation of quotas should have given independent producers the opportunity to boost British output. But the decision of the 'majors' to use the reduced studio space to make costly films with a view to penetrating the American market prevented that increase in output. As a direct result, exhibitors were often unable to meet their quota requirement of 12.5% and this did sometimes lead to court action. But the combines, through their control of each element of the trade, were able to direct what films could be made and where they would be shown.

This situation caused concern both inside and outside the industry, and in 1943 the government set up a committee of enquiry under the chairmanship of Albert Palache to investigate the development of monopoly within the industry. The Palache Committee's Report, *Tendencies to Monopoly in the Cinematograph Film Industry*, was published in 1944. However, some questioned its timing; after all, the government was more or less in control of the industry via the Ministry of Information and was enjoying a considerable annual windfall from entertainments tax.

The report was the first comprehensive review of the industry and how it worked. It criticised the concentration of power in the combines, unfair charges by distributors (who often took 35% of the box-office receipts), the risk to future production by leaving control in the hands of two groups and the danger of continuing American domination. It also called for legal limits to be imposed on the number of cinemas controlled by the major circuits. The report called monopoly 'a threat to the future prospects of an independent and unfettered British film industry' and emphasised the point: 'In our opinion, a healthy British film industry can be built up from the remnants existing at present only on condition that independent production remains in being and is properly safeguarded' (Palache Committee 1944). The implication was clear: the government should support the independent producer.

The government was also called on to establish a film finance corporation to oversee the continuity of funding and establish a distribution organisation to handle 'independent' films on merit alone. An overseas subsidiary was proposed to handle British films abroad. The report also suggested that the allocation of studio space should be decided by a tribunal, as would terms of film hire, distribution and circuit expansion. (In 1944 Rank and ABPC agreed not to increase their cinemas without Board of Trade consent.)

The report found a 'definitive tendency towards monopoly' – probably duopoly would have been more accurate – and all aspects of the industry were responsible for 'undesirable practices in

restraint of trade'; 'the preponderating influence of American interests in this country' was to be dealt with by legislation, if necessary
(ibid.). These comments were directed at the exhibitors and distributors, but there was a suggestion in the body of the report that Rank
and ABPC's production decisions could be affected by US con-
siderations.

The trade press reacted against the threat of government intervention and an editorial in the *Financial Times* supported this view:

> Not all of the recommendations will commend themselves, least
> of all to the big film producers, since the element of control or
> compulsion might well be regarded as unduly stressed. . . .
>
> Who better than the industry can decide, apart from the
> benevolent propaganda value of documentaries and education-
> als, the most worth-while types of films from the standpoint of
> the box-office? Financially successful films are essential to a
> sound industry at home and vital if any sort of progress is to be
> achieved in the development of exports of British films, for it is
> this latter aspect, it must be assumed, which will influence any
> government action that may ultimately be contemplated.
> (*Financial Times*, 3 August 1944)

The end of the war was approaching and little action was taken,
apart from the circuit limitation agreement and a promise from the
various trade bodies to tackle their internal problems; and, in particular, the Palache Committee's explicit criticism of Rank's planned
expansion into the world market was to be ignored in the immediate
post-war era.

CHAPTER 5

The Post-war Years: 1945–51

'On the industrial front the post-war years are plagued with troubles; the independent producer, though he has gained in authority, is still in doubt about his future, and spends more time raising money than making films. In its financing methods the industry is as unbending as ever, affairs are always moving towards a crisis' (Betts 1974, p. 215).

In July 1945 a Labour government was elected and it had a considerable impact on the future of the British film industry, both in terms of its early support for Rank's expansionary production plans and the measures that were introduced to assist, or protect, the trade. The government launched its 'peaceful revolution' and there was a mood of optimism in the country; and film-makers had many reasons to be hopeful. The war years had seen the success of numerous British films at home and abroad, particularly in the US; cinema attendances were booming and box-office receipts stood at record levels; studio space was again available and wartime restrictions were being lifted, albeit gradually. The Labour government, whose members were generally more friendly towards the industry, appreciated the need to boost production and penetrate the American market; and the man to achieve this breakthrough was Rank. The last thing anyone wanted was a collapse in film production of the kind witnessed in the 1920s.

EXHIBITION AND DISTRIBUTION

At the end of the war the three main circuits, Gaumont-British, ABPC and Odeon, still dominated the exhibition business, but the Granada group expanded from 35 cinemas in 1945 to 56 in 1948 and the Essoldo chain grew rapidly in the immediate post-war era (PEP 1952, p. 93). However, what marked this period was the beginning of a decline in cinema attendances and the consequent fall in box-office receipts. According to the relevant White Papers, in 1945 the annual expenditure on cinema-going in the UK was £117 million, and by 1950 it had fallen to £107 million. Meanwhile cinema admissions fell from 1,585 million in 1945 to 1,395 million in 1950; the peak year was 1946 with 1,635 million admissions (British Film Institute 2001, p. 34). The implementation of the Eady Plan in 1950, which raised cinema seat prices, was just one of the reasons for the downturn throughout the 1950s and beyond.

The distribution market was still in thrall to the American companies and the leading British competitors in 1945 were GFD, Associated British–Pathé and British Lion; and in 1951 the position was virtually unchanged. The British renters handled just over 26% of all the long films registered and 37% of British films. The seven American 'majors' (Columbia, Twentieth Century–Fox, MGM, Warners, Paramount, RKO Radio and United Artists) distributed 42% of all long films, British and foreign. Within the period, the number of films handled by GFD fell from 55 in 1949 to 23 in 1951 as a direct result of the cutback in Rank's production programme (PEP 1952, p. 225).

PRODUCTION: FIRST REEL

By 1946 Alexander Korda had left MGM and reformed London Film Productions as a private company with a capital of £825,000 (Threadgall 1994, p. 35). In that year London Films acquired British Lion Film Corporation, which owned Beaconsfield Studios, 50% of Worton Hall and was an important production/distribution company. Later in 1946 a 74% stake in Sound City (Films) Ltd, which had studios at Shepperton, was purchased for £380,000 (PEP 1952, p. 94) and the remaining 50% of Worton Hall was bought for a mixture of cash (£80,000) and shares in British Lion Studio Company. Korda now had eight stages and 11,000 square feet of studio floor space available for production (ibid., p. 94); only Rank's facilities were greater. A successful rights issue in mid June 1946, based on British Lion's healthy dividend record, raised £1 million and at the same time Korda negotiated a deal with Twentieth Century–Fox to distribute his films in America. Over the next few years he was to produce some of the most memorable films of the post-war era, including *The Fallen Idol* (1948) and *The Third Man* (1949).

Although ABPC's studios at Elstree did not reopen until 1948, the company was in the news in February 1946 when it was revealed that Warner Brothers had bought a further 1 million shares for £1.125 million. This purchase gave them a 37.5% stake in the issued share capital. The trustees of ABPC pointed out that the voting rights were unaffected. However, misgivings were loudly voiced and Warner's increased holding did appear to ignore the recommendations of the Palache Committee. (In the immediate post-war period ABPC was very successful, largely due to the boom in attendances at its ABC cinemas. From 1944–45 to 1949–50, gross annual dividend payments averaged 23%; in the peak financial year of 1946–47, 30% was paid.)

The consolidation of his empire in the early 1940s and the subsequent backing of many successful wartime productions suggested that Rank was the man to build on the industry's newly-won importance. He had the financial resources to back his ambition to penetrate the American market and distributors – Eagle-Lion Films Inc. and Universal-International – to handle his films in the US. But the omens were not good. Since 1944 Rank's GCFC had been losing money on production; in that year losses totalled over £179,000; in 1945 they had risen to £378,293, and between 1945 and 1946 the loss had grown to a staggering £1.667 million (ibid., p. 97). Rank had suffered mixed fortunes in America. *Henry V* (1944) had been a commercial success there, and although *Caesar and Cleopatra* (1945), which cost a phenomenal £1.25 million to make, is often regarded as folly on a grand scale, it took £1.79 million plus at the US box-office (Macnab 1993, p. 101). In 1948 another 'folly', *The Red Shoes*, costing £700,000, was to be relatively unsuccessful in Britain, but went on to gross $5 million in America over a six-year period (ibid., p. 109).

Olivier's *Hamlet* (1948) also succeeded through US art-house distribution. However, other films of the period did not, including *Great Expectations* (1946) and Rank's attempt at a British musical, *London Town* (1947), was a million-pound disaster. By 1947 it was clear that many Rank films were not getting mass distribution in the US, and if they did, the costs involved cut back on their potential profitability; and in the summer of that year, the government was to take action which would confound the industry.

INTERVENTION: FIRST REEL

In 1947 the government faced a balance of payments crisis. There had been a drain on the country's gold and dollar reserves, and measures were introduced to deal with the situation. These included controls on the import of food, petrol rationing and the banning of foreign travel, except for business purposes. The Chancellor also imposed an 'ad valorem' duty of 75% on the value of all imported films. As we saw in Chapter 4, annual remittances to the United States were restricted between 1940 and 1942. Blocked funds were released in 1943 and by 1947 the annual payment had reached approximately £17.5 million. Given the fragility of the post-war economy, the government stated that it would not make payments on this scale for the exhibition of American films in British cinemas. The Dalton duty, named after the Chancellor of the Exchequer, now appears to have been conceived in haste, and its implications were not fully considered by the government.

The announcement of the duty came as Rank had begun to see signs of cordiality on the part of the US industry. That now dissolved: Hollywood could not afford to lose 25% of its annual overseas revenue and immediately suspended the export of its films to the UK (*Cinema*, 20 August 1947). The British exhibitors supported the American stance, fearing that a lack of new films would hit box-office takings, and they also resented the fact that there had been no consultation on the matter. The exhibitors' quota for 1947 was 20% (for British films) and in 1948 it was set to rise to 25%; the remaining percentages were accounted for by US productions. If the problem was not resolved, the exhibitors argued, the downturn would be rapid. In the meantime they relied on reissues and extended runs.

The government regarded the situation as one in which British producers could expand their output. It was a somewhat ingenuous view and many, including Balcon, were sceptical. True, our main competitor had been lost, but the American market was now closed to British films; and British output would not be able to make up the loss of Hollywood films – cinemas would close. Rank, however, responded positively:

> In October, 1947, he announced a hugely ambitious film production programme. Over the next twelve months, the Rank Organization undertook to make 43 features, at a combined cost of £9,250,000, while continuing apace with its children's films, animation, newsreels and 'B' pictures. (Macnab 1993, p. 182)

He also reorganised his interests: Odeon Theatres Ltd became the parent company through which activities were channelled and the Odeon and Gaumont circuits were merged into the Circuits Management Association (CMA).

The Labour government quickly realised that the duty was not working and in March 1948 an Anglo-American film agreement was reached. The main provisions were that the duty would be scrapped and for the two years starting on 14 June 1948, $17 million (£4.25 million) could be remitted annually to the US. It was possible to increase this figure by the amount earned by British films in America. Earnings not returned in this way could be reinvested in the British film industry (even cinemas, subject to the agreement of a joint control committee).

The President of the Board of Trade, Harold Wilson, estimated that the agreement would save around $33 million annually (PEP 1952, p. 101). The Dalton duty now appears a rash measure, and if it had continued the effect on the British box office would have been severe. The film industry could not expect to remain aloof from the economic pressures of the time, but consultations should have taken place with the trade. Instead, a short-term expedient backfired.

By 1948 Rank had already increased output and ABPC resumed production at a revamped Elstree. But the independent companies, such as British Lion, were undercapitalised and financial help from the City of London was not forthcoming. (Many institutional invest-ors had long memories and gloomily recalled the slump of the late 1930s.) Collapse was again predicted and the government realised that survival rather than expansion was now the question. Con-sequently, two measures were undertaken: the introduction of the Cinematograph Films Act of 1948 and the establishment of the National Film Finance Corporation.

The 1948 act was significant in that the renters' quota was aban-doned as a result of the 1947 General Agreement on Tariffs and Trade (GATT), which only allowed 'screen' quotas. The exhibitors' quota was increased to 45% (it was reduced to 30% in 1950, remaining at that level until it was abolished in 1983) on long films (from 25%) and 25% for the supporting, 'short' programme (22.5%). The quotas were to be fixed on an annual basis by the Board of Trade. This huge increase in the exhibitors' quota could be seen as obvious protection-ism, but the majority opinion within the trade was that British pro-ducers would be unable to fill the higher figure.

The National Film Finance Corporation (NFFC) was created in October 1948. The President of the Board of Trade believed that, without Treasury help, there was a risk of British film production ceasing (apart from Rank). Initially, the NFFC had a life of five years and the government contributed £5 million. (This sum was raised to £6 million in 1950.) Many believed that the scheme was introduced to bail out Korda's British Lion – which was to lose £2.187 million on production in the 1948 fiscal year (Threadgall 1994, p. 59) – and Del Guidice's Two Cities company. Korda did in fact receive £1 million, later increased to £3 million, but Del Guidice was given nothing. By March 1951 the NFFC had spent over £5 million on 101 films and encouraged new companies specialising in the training of tech-nicians as well as production groups. The independents became important during this period, with first feature output leaping by nearly 70% between 1948 and 1951 (PEP 1952, p. 269).

PRODUCTION: SECOND REEL

The year 1947–48 was the best in terms of film production since the heady days of 1937–38. One hundred and seventy British 'long' films were completed – compared with 83 in 1945–46, 107 in 1946–47 – and the gross value of production was £19.319 million – compared with £7.163 million in 1937 (PEP 1952, p. 96). First feature output increased and the number of people employed, technical and administrative, rose during the same period by around 85%. Rank provided 32 features in 1948 and experienced a loss on production of £3.350 million, a figure that would have risen to £4.646 million but for a change in the basis of film valuation. The bank overdraft stood at £16.5 million and the group had £14.5 million of long-term debentures at the end of the 1948–49 financial year. Equity dividends would not be resumed until the 1953–54 year. There was no option but to curtail production. (At one point it was thought that it might have to be abandoned completely.) In his statement to Odeon Theatres Ltd shareholders (for the financial year to 25 June 1949) Rank admitted that his plans had been too ambitious and many of the films produced 'were not of a quality to ensure even reasonable returns'. In addition, British films had to compete with the log-jam of Hollywood features that were released after the Anglo-American agreement was ratified. Retrenchment was now the creed at the Rank Organisation with John Davis, the managing director, assuming greater influence; it was a policy of restraint as opposed to expansion.

INTERVENTION: SECOND REEL

The year 1949 has been called 'the year when everything went wrong' (Oakley 1964, p. 194). Box-office takings fell to £105 million, from £121 million in 1946, and there was a decline of over 50% in people actually employed in British studios. Also, Shepherd's Bush Studios were sold to the BBC, a symbolic disposal if nothing else; others closed, including Islington and Twickenham. There were fears of a complete breakdown in production. But 1949 also saw the release of three Ealing comedies that were to become classics of British cinema: *Kind Hearts and Coronets*, *Whisky Galore* and *Passport to Pimlico*. At least Ealing got something right in that year.

In November 1948 Harold Wilson set up two committees: the Working Party on Film Production Costs was chaired by Sir George

Gator and the Committee on the Distribution and Exhibition of Cinematograph Films was chaired by Sir Arnold Plant, following the death of the original chairman, Lord Portal. Their reports were published a year later.

The Gator Report found 'extravagance and unreality' among producers and the lack of planning was described as 'the most serious deficiency in the industry'. Accepting that, for most films, overseas revenue was likely to be minimal, the report suggested that unless producers recovered a high proportion of their costs in the home market, the establishment of a viable industry for the long term was a pipe dream.

The Plant Report highlighted the rigid nature of the exhibition and distribution businesses, but came out in favour of changes in trade practices rather than structural alterations to the industry itself. The report was very critical of entertainments tax, calling it a 'serious handicap' to producers. After its deduction, the report argued, the share of box-office receipts was not large enough to allow exhibitors to pay British producers a decent return on their films.

Subsequently a Trade Committee report, which accepted the main contention of the Plant Report, i.e. the rigidity of exhibition and distribution arrangements, was submitted to the Board of Trade in June 1950. The same month saw the announcement of the British Film Production Fund, or Eady Plan as it became known (named after Sir Wilfred Eady, Second Secretary of the Treasury). Its aim was to subsidise producers, and in exchange for adjustments to entertainments tax, exhibitors could increase some seat prices and pay a levy into the fund. It was anticipated that tax receipts would fall by £300,000 annually and the changes would provide the industry with £3 million per year, one-half of which would be paid to the producers directly (PEP 1952, p. 127).

Entertainments tax was abolished on seats up to and including 7d; above 7d and up to and including 12s 6d the tax was reduced by ½d; on seat prices between 1s 6d and 3s 9d tax adjustments were made to allow a 1d increase in price of which ½d was taken in tax (ibid., pp. 127–28). In exchange, the exhibitors had to pay ¼d into the fund for each ticket sold and, with little dissent, they agreed to the scheme.

It has been estimated that if the fund had been in existence for the whole of 1950, it would have given producers £1.25 million, on top of their receipts of £3.5 million in that year (ibid., p. 129). But producers would still have suffered an overall loss of approximately £2.75 million. In 1951 there were further calls for concessions on entertainments tax which would allow the fund to be increased. Hugh Gaitskell, the Chancellor of the Exchequer, did not respond and his Budget actually proposed increases in the tax, on a rising scale. In return the Treasury would forego ½d per ticket. Around £10 million was expected to be raised, with 75% going to the Treasury and 25% to the industry. A greater part of the industry's percentage should be passed on to the producers, the Chancellor suggested.

The industry baulked at the Budget proposals and a compromise was reached involving variable payments on different seat prices; seats up to and including 7d stayed tax-free and the tax on 1s seats fell by 1d. The outcome was that the public would pay an extra £12.5 million per year at the box office (£6.5 million to the Treasury, £2.3 million to the producers and £3.7 million to the exhibitors). The £2.3 million to the producers would be on top of the sum raised by the initial ¼d levy (ibid., p. 130).

The Eady Plan, as adapted, was a positive move to help British producers and without it the industry might well have collapsed. (The new plan was expected to last until August 1954, but it continued until 1985.) Its lasting success was dependent on there being no fall in attendances; however, by 1951 attendances had decreased, on a weekly basis, by around 5 million since the 1946 peak.

Following the strong performance in the year 1947–48, the number of British 'long' films fell to 120 in 1948–49, rose to 132 in 1949–50, but declined again to 125 in 1950–51. Within these individual figures, however, can be found an increase in first features: 71, 93 and 75 for the three years concerned (ibid., p. 269). NFFC funding helped considerably, especially at a time when Rank was cutting back; and independent production was boosted as a corollary.

Given the post-war background and the Labour administration's extensive programme of reform, it is perhaps surprising that the film industry was the subject of so much debate and legislation. The Cinematograph Films Act of 1948, the formation of the NFFC, the Gator and Plant Reports and the introduction of the Eady Plan in 1950, all showed a responsiveness on the part of the government to the plight of the industry, especially the producers. Unfortunately, it only tinkered with the 'iniquitous' entertainments tax, which was to remain in force until 1960. An opportunity had been missed.

In 1951 the Conservatives returned to power. They found an industry that was protected by quotas and partially financed through the NFFC and the Eady Levy; it operated in the shadow of American competition and was itself unable to break into the US market. And the industry was faced with falling attendances, a trend that was to gain momentum as the 1950s progressed.

CHAPTER 6

The 1950s

During the 1950s *The Seventh Veil* was shown on British television. Shortly afterwards it was reported that cinema attendances throughout the country had dropped by 15% on that particular evening (Hill 1959). It is possible that many viewers were misled by the film's title, but the incident serves as a useful illustration of the threat posed by television in that decade.

EXHIBITION

In 1950 the average weekly admissions to cinemas stood at 27 million; by 1959 the figure had fallen to under 12 million. The number of cinemas also fell, from 4,600 (seating 4.25 million) in 1950 to 3,600 (seating 3.5 million) in 1959 (Oakley 1964, p. 208). The decline in cinemas was happening at a slower pace, but the smaller, independent theatres were suffering from a combination of rising costs, falling revenue and the burden of entertainments tax. Yet, despite the fall in weekly admissions, gross box-office takings rose from £105.2 million in 1950 to £110 million in 1954 due to increased seat prices, and even in 1955 (£105.8 million) and 1956 (£104.2 million) gross takings were only marginally lower. By 1957, however, they had collapsed to £92.7 million, the lowest annual total since 1942 (PEP 1958, pp. 135–36), and higher seat prices were no longer able to compensate for the decline in admissions. Throughout the decade the exhibitors' quota, 30% for British films, remained unchanged. After allowing for relief, the average was just above 25%, and the main circuits often exceeded 30% during the 1950s (ibid., p. 162).

In essence, the 1950s saw little variation in the dominance of the Rank/ABC duopoly. Odeon and Gaumont-British were owned by Rank (Twentieth Century–Fox's stake was finally bought out for £4 million in 1961) and, together with ABC (ABPC acquired Warner Brothers' 37.5% interest for £2.5 million in the early 1960s), the three main circuits controlled 950 cinemas in the mid 1950s. They represented one-third of the total seating capacity and 44% of the annual box-office receipts (Manvell 1955, p. 214). The duopoly also owned some two-thirds of the 'first run' cinemas in the West End of London. There were shifts, though, among the medium-large circuits. In 1951 the four main companies were Essoldo, King, Granada and SM Associated. Essoldo had grown rapidly since the war, and during the 1950s the company acquired the bulk of SM Associated's cinemas. Between 1951 and 1957 the number of its cinemas doubled from 92 to 183 and it almost doubled its seating capacity to 195,000 (PEP 1958, p. 161). Leeds-based Star had 51 cinemas in 1951 with 38,000 seats; six years later it had 114 (88,000 seats). In the early 1970s Star was involved in an abortive bid for British Lion. King (80 cinemas and 85,000 seats) and Granada (56 cinemas and 85,000 seats) maintained their status in this grouping, which in 1957 accounted for 10% of the cinemas in the UK and 11% of the total seating capacity (ibid., p. 159).

By the mid 1950s the exhibitors started to feel the real impact of television. But it was not a specifically British problem: audiences were declining throughout the world and the US industry had experienced the initial effect of television on attendances in the late 1940s. In Britain, as we have seen, audiences began to wane as early as 1947 and the rise in seat prices as a consequence of the Eady Plan was the principal reason. (The quality of the programmes offered was another.)

At the end of 1947 there were 18,000 TV and radio licences held in Britain; in 1960 there were 10 million plus (Oakley 1964, p. 208). Coronation year, 1953, is often mentioned as the year in which television made its breakthrough, and many households undoubtedly acquired a television set to watch the event. But other commentators saw 1955 as a more significant year as it marked the launch of commercial television. In fact, Lord Rank estimated that in its first six months of operation cinema admissions fell by 10% (Rank

Organisation Annual Report 1956, p. 21). Later Lord Bernstein, chairman of Granada, commented:

> During the immediate post-war years when the BBC only were operating, the effect on audience attendances was minimal, but with the advent of commercial television and the resultant choice of programmes, admissions declined sharply.
>
> The older age group who had been accustomed to attending cinemas regularly once or twice a week stayed at home, with the result that audiences which at one time prior to the advent of TV were composed of people from, say, 10 to 65, were after the introduction of commercial TV composed of the age group 10 to 25. (Betts 1973, p. 327)

John Spraos, in his book *The Decline of the Cinema,* argued against the view that commercial television in itself had made matters worse for the industry. He suggested that:

> The important factors through which television has damaged the cinema must therefore be presumed to be (1) the convenience of home entertainment rather than the specific type of entertainment; (2) the pre-emption of a certain part of the weekly income for HP payments or rent on the set; (3) the fact that each visit to the cinema has a price whereas 'switching on' is virtually costless. (Spraos 1962, p. 29)

But he did agree that there was a 'sharp steepening of the decline in cinema attendances after 1955' and pointed out that the following year saw cinema closures gain momentum. Also, there is evidence that the growth in ownership of TV sets among the working classes accelerated at this time; and the working classes had been the main patrons of the cinema throughout its history. Whatever the reasons, the downturn was severe – in 1955 annual cinema admissions were 893.2 million but in 1960 they were 375 million (figures from the Board of Trade).

As well as television, the exhibitors had to face the problem of film supply. In 1950 the US government invoked antitrust legislation which effectively ended the vertically integrated structure of the leading American film companies. Hollywood studios no longer had a financial incentive in making films to show in cinemas that they did not own. As a result, production was cut back and between 1952 and 1962 the number of feature films made in the US fell from 278 to 138 per year (Threadgall 1994, p. 97). This lower output caused British exhibitors considerable planning problems.

Faced with dwindling audiences at home and abroad, the Hollywood studios introduced various gimmicks to attract patrons such as 3D and, more successfully, CinemaScope. CinemaScope was pioneered by Twentieth Century–Fox and others followed suit, such as Paramount with VistaVision and Warner Brothers with Warnerscope. The larger CinemaScope screen lent itself to spectacular films – the first in this format was *The Robe* (1953) – but British exhibitors were hit by the cost of installing the new equipment. (The Rank Organisation objected to the extra costs involved and fell out with Fox as a result; later a dispute over hire terms led to the boycott of Rank cinemas by Fox between 1956 and 1958.) The resistance was short-lived, however, and gradually cinemas throughout Britain converted to the new screens and sound systems.

In 1956 the Rank Organisation closed 79 cinemas and the following year ABC shut 65. By 1958 the startling news was revealed that 25% of the country's cinemas were running at a loss; and in that year another threat from television emerged – its appetite for old films. ABC, one of the new commercial stations, bought 25 Korda films and the BBC purchased 100 features from RKO (Hill 1959). This was regarded as the ultimate folly by the industry and the response took the form of the Film Industry Defence Organisation (FIDO). Its purpose was to initiate a boycott against the films of producers and/or distributors who sold their films to television. An agency was established to buy the rights to British films and it was funded via a levy of one farthing per seat in cinemas throughout the country. Some cinemas were excluded – those earning less than £200 per week at the box office, around 1,800 (ibid.). It was expected that the scheme would raise between £500,000 and £750,000 per year.

At first the exhibitors were wary of FIDO, sensing that, once again, they were expected to foot the bill. Sir Michael Balcon was strongly against the organisation but his position was somewhat compromised by the sale of Ealing films to TV. But ATV, another commercial venture, did go so far as to seek legal opinion on the grounds of restrictive practice. However, the protests came to nothing, and in its first year of operation FIDO claimed to have prevented thousands of films being offered to the television companies due to its vigilance. The exhibitors paid their levies, albeit reluctantly, and a short-term objective was achieved. Eventually, though, the scheme was abandoned.

A further irony was that Rank, with a 37.67% stake in Southern Television, Sir Philip Warter and Associated British Picture Corporation via the Midlands-based ABC, and the Bernsteins through Granada in the North of England, all became prominent figures in the development of commercial television. Quite simply, they read the runes and acted appropriately – as shrewd businessmen.

The 1950s witnessed the closure of 1,500 cinemas, nearly one-third of the total, but the decline had no effect on the structure of exhibition. Rank and ABPC still controlled this aspect of the industry and the success or failure of any British film was determined by their decisions regarding circuit release.

While the ABPC corporate structure remained unchanged, Rank reorganised the network of private companies that controlled his group. In 1953 United Artists sold its stake in Odeon Cinema Holdings Ltd which, in turn, owned Odeon Theatres Ltd and was controlled by Rank himself. The changes were motivated by Rank's desire to keep the group in British hands (Twentieth Century–Fox still had its large shareholding at this time). A new company was set up to retain voting control, and dividends on Rank's former holdings were paid into a charitable trust. Neither Rank nor his wife had any financial or voting interest in the new concern (PEP 1958, p. 144). At the 1955 AGM, the name of Odeon Theatres Ltd was changed to the Rank Organisation Ltd.

Rank's overdraft had been reduced to £4 million in 1954 and cinema attendances were up in that year. In 1955 Rank's cinemas made operating profits of around £3.5 million, matching the previous peak year of 1951. But attendances continued their inexorable decline, and in 1956 John Davis made the acquisition that was to transform the Rank Organisation, Rank Xerox Ltd. By 1969 it was providing 90% of the group's pre-tax profits.

In 1958 the Rank Organisation amalgamated its two releasing circuits, Odeon and Gaumont, into a single entity – the Rank 'release'. The reasons for this move included the current shortage of, mainly

American, films and the increased bargaining power of the single 'release'. ABC could not compete at this level. John Spraos has suggested that ABC was probably equal to Odeon and superior to Gaumont (Spraos 1962, p. 94). The third grouping – small and independent cinemas – came under the broad heading of a 'National Circuit', working among themselves to pick up films rejected by Rank and ABC. More closures were certain to come as a consequence of Rank's strategy.

The state of the industry at the end of the 1950s probably made the directors of Associated British Picture Corporation Ltd thankful that they had invested in commercial television. In the year to 31 March 1959 the company achieved record pre-tax profits of £4.745 million and paid a gross dividend of 60%. ABC Television Limited contributed 56% of the corporation's trading profits of £3.05 million with the balance coming from production, distribution and exhibition. Elstree Studios had a good year, being fully utilised, and the chairman, Sir Philip Warter, pointed out at the AGM that ABC Cinemas had seen attendances 'better than the national average' and improved their overall position.

By the late 1950s admissions had fallen still further: around 11.5 million was the weekly average, less than one-third of the 1950 total. Rank owned 372 cinemas in 1960 and ABC 266 of some 2,800 that remained open. Their control of exhibition was to remain intact throughout the 1960s.

This period did end with a triumph of sorts for the hard-pressed exhibitors. They had become more active in their opposition to the despised entertainments tax, and consistent lobbying resulted in concessions on the part of the government. In 1959 it had fallen to 15% and the following year it was abolished. From 1950 to 1957 a total of £280 million was contributed by the exhibitors to the Exchequer, some 30% of gross takings of £845 million. But the sting in the tail for many exhibitors was that the end of the duty would be offset by falling admissions. On the latter point, Mr Spraos estimated that a decline of 15–25% was likely over the next ten years (to 1970). In fact, the downturn was far greater than predicted: in 1970 cinema admissions totalled 193 million, a fall of 62.5% on the 1960 figure.

DISTRIBUTION

As with exhibition there was little change in the overall structure of the business. In 1951 the ten leading distributors handled a total of 379 long films, of which 58 were British; by 1958 that total had decreased slightly to 360 but the number of British films distributed had risen to 84. The 1951 total represented 57% of all long films registered (the British figure was 45% of the home output); in 1958 the corresponding percentages were 64 and 62. The major British renters, Rank, AB Pathé and British Lion, offered a total of 149 films in 1951 (47 British) and 117 in 1958 (49 British). The seven American companies significantly increased the number of British films they were handling, from 11 in 1951 to 35 in 1958 (PEP 1958, p. 164). However, this was largely due to the growth in Anglo-American productions and the fact that MGM had begun to distribute Ealing films.

Within the American group (Twentieth Century–Fox, Columbia, MGM, RKO-Radio, Warners, Paramount and United Artists) there was movement in the 1950s. Columbia was the largest US distributor in 1951 with 75 films, but by 1958 United Artists was handling 58 films against Columbia's 51 (ibid., p. 164). In 1953 UA had sold its interests in Odeon Cinema Holdings and concentrated on helping independent producers; this coincided with the start of the movement into television by the US majors.

By the end of this period the seven US companies were distributing 43% of all long films. Rank distributed the bulk of Universal-International's films and the three leading British renters distributed 21% of all long films registered and 36% of British films. Among other British renters in the late 1950s, Anglo-Amalgamated, Eros and Gala were handling over 20 films each annually (ibid., p. 165).

Although the distribution structure was unaltered, the effect of dwindling audiences and cinema closures did lead many within the trade to question the status quo of one or two programmes a week in British cinemas. The implication was that a popular film would not achieve its full financial potential if its 'run' was limited to one week. The 'extended run' argument was heard in the 1950s, but it would be some years before circumstances forced change.

PRODUCTION

In 1950 the UK produced 125 feature films and in 1959 the figure was 122 (British Film Institute 2001, p. 30). The average per year over the decade was just above 124. Hollywood's output fell during this period and many US independent producers came to Britain to make films at a lower overall cost. The American majors, including MGM, Fox, Warner Brothers and RKO, also arrived or returned in the early 1950s, recognising an opportunity to spend 'blocked earnings' and achieve the British quota; they also gained from the levy on box-office receipts. Films such as RKO's *Treasure Island* (1951) were commercially successful and helped to establish a hold that would consolidate in the coming years: by 1956 one-third of British films were wholly or partly financed by US capital (Oakley 1964, p. 208).

The Rank Organisation had ended the 1940s with a hefty £16 million overdraft and John Davis, the group's managing, director, introduced a radical cost-cutting programme which included a £150,000 ceiling on feature film budgets. These measures did not endear him to the film-makers, but they worked, and by 1954 the total debt had fallen to £4 million. In that year the group made a profit of nearly £1 million on film production and, significantly, around 50% of this figure came from abroad. But it was a blip and in 1955 only 10% of profits came from production and distribution.

Apart from the cost-cutting exercise, there had been a shift of emphasis within the Rank Organisation and the new credo was 'family entertainment'. This proved successful in the mid 1950s with the Norman Wisdom comedies and the *Doctor* series. Later the *Carry On* films were to become commercial hits in both the UK and the US. But the closure of Denham Studios in 1952, resulting in open warfare with the Association of Cine Technicians (ACT), and the group's concentration on the refurbishment of theatres, cinema management training courses and, more significantly, the purchase of Xerox in 1956 convinced many within the industry that Rank's days as a prominent film-maker were over. In fact, by the end of the decade, film production was barely profitable and the future lay with Rank Xerox.

The share stake that Warner Brothers had bought from John Maxwell's estate in 1945 was to have an effect on ABPC's distribution and exhibition divisions as well as production. (In essence, Warner Brothers would distribute ABPC's films in its 800 US cinemas and ABPC would show Warner Brothers films on its circuit.) Elstree Studios were reconstructed, opening in 1948, and by the early 1950s international productions such as *Captain Horatio Hornblower*, with American stars, were being made at Elstree under the watchful eye of Robert Clark, another Scot and a protégé of Maxwell. But intrinsically British films were also produced successfully: *The Dam Busters* and *Ice Cold in Alex* are two examples.

However, the board of ABPC decided that commercial television offered exciting investment opportunities and ABC Television was awarded the contracts for the Midlands and Northern programmes on Saturdays and Sundays. Teddington Studios was the base and Elstree began to make television productions in tandem with feature films. It was a strategy that would achieve solid financial rewards.

A decade that had begun so promisingly for Ealing Studios with films such as *The Blue Lamp* (1950) and *The Lavender Hill Mob* (1951) was soon to turn sour. As early as 1952 the studios faced difficulties, largely due to undercapitalisation, and by 1955 debt had become unmanageable; assets were sold, including the studios (the BBC bought them for £300,000). Michael Balcon entered into a production agreement with MGM, but the sale of Ealing was effectively the end of his career as a leading producer.

BRITISH LION

At the beginning of the 1950s, Alexander Korda's British Lion was second only to the Rank Organisation in terms of studio space and facilities. There had been critical and commercial successes such as *The Fallen Idol* (1948) and *The Third Man* (1949), but high production losses began to accumulate and the position worsened when Republic, the US producer, ended its relationship with the company. (Since 1935 British Lion had handled the release of Republic's films in the UK.)

Korda had borrowed £3 million from the The National Film Finance Corporation (NFFC) in the late 1940s, but by the financial year 1952–53, when a loss of over £150,000 was recorded, the total debt had reached £2.227 million. The NFFC called in its loan in June 1954 and a receiver and manager were appointed. During this period, successful films such as *The African Queen, The Sound Barrier* and *Richard III* were made at the company's Shepperton studios but unfortunately film-making talent was not matched by business acumen.

Korda's downfall was all the more striking since British Lion had been a major beneficiary of the Eady Levy. In the first three years of its operation, to August 1953, British Lion received £933,622, Gaumont Film Distributors £1,741,683 and Associated British–Pathé £748,122 (Threadgall 1994, pp. 64–65). In 1957 the British Film Fund Agency replaced the original British Film Production Fund (BFP) and Customs & Excise undertook the collection of payments from the exhibitors. But falling admissions meant a lower return and gradually the benefits to British producers became negligible. (In the early days of the scheme, US financiers who had backed 'British' films were able to take their share of the levy without any obligation to reinvest even part of it in the British industry.)

Following Korda's departure a new company, British Lion Films Limited, was created in January 1955 with an authorised capital of £1 million in ordinary shares of £1 each. The company issued 600,000 shares to acquire the assets of the old company. The new shares were accepted by the NFFC 'in satisfaction of its debenture debt of £3 million and of the advance of the £569,000 of new money' (PEP 1958, p. 147). The objective was to continue the distribution side of the business, and although the new company owned Shepperton, it would not make films itself but hire out the studios to independent producers. Another distribution company, Lion International Films, was also established to handle overseas sales. David Kingsley, the managing director of the NFFC, was appointed a director of the studio company – he later became managing director – and the intention was to keep a firm grip on the new company's activities. The NFFC recovered over £1.5 million in the next couple of years (Threadgall 1994, p. 89). Experienced film-makers such as Sidney Gilliatt, Frank Launder and the Boulting brothers were appointed to the board in 1958 and although the financial position did improve, the profit record was still erratic.

Year to	Profit or loss (£)
31.03.57	17,228
31.03.58	−337,114
31.03.59	−153,354
31.03.60	100,000

Bryanston Films was created under the chairmanship of Michael Balcon with a capital of £1 million and important investors such as the Rank Organisation and Lloyds Bank Ltd. Their films were distributed through British Lion and many of the productions shot at Shepperton. It was an exciting venture and *Saturday Night and Sunday Morning* (1959) an early, resounding success. As the 1960s approached there was a degree of optimism in the air.

THE NFFC

Towards the end of the decade, the National Film Finance Corporation came under fire and an editorial in the Summer/Autumn issue of *Sight & Sound* discussed the implications of the NFFC's 1958 annual report which showed a loss of £222,367, almost double the 1957 figure. The *Times* was particularly damning in its criticism of the organisation and suggested that it was 'time to call a halt'. The independent producers were quick to enter the lists, pointing out that during its ten-year existence the NFFC had lost an annual amount of some £127,000, but during the same period the British film industry had contributed £300 million in entertainments tax; and between 1950 and 1956, 56% of British first features released on the three main circuits were at least partly financed by the NFFC (PEP 1958, p. 146).

As we explained in Chapter 5, the NFFC was created in 1948 under Board of Trade sponsorship and granted the power to give loans to independent producers. By March 1951 it had spent over £5.5 million on 101 films (Betts 1973, p. 221). In terms of its commercial viability, the NFFC was hamstrung by the British Lion loan from the beginning. It had a responsibility to avoid making losses, but many of the independent productions involved a high degree of risk that would not have been countenanced by Rank or ABPC.

In 1951 the NFFC had launched a group production scheme; in fact, there were three groups, one in association with the Rank Organisation called British Film Makers Ltd, based at Pinewood. GFD handled the distribution and provided a 70% guarantee on which a bank loan could be raised. The remaining 30% came from the NFFC and it retained a controlling interest in the share capital of the company. A similar arrangement was made with ABPC at Elstree and produced five films. Both groups were wound up by the end of 1952. However, the third group, Group 3, continued until 1955, making 22 features and in this case the costs were split 50:50 between ABFD, who handled distribution, and the NFFC. Overall the group scheme could have been an interesting experiment if it had been given the time to develop.

Following publication of the 1958 accounts, various suggestions were put forward, including a proposal that star names should be paid a percentage of the profits rather than lavish fees. Also the existing format of 'front money' (the distributor's guarantee) and 'end money' (the 30% cost of production which the producer has to find) should be reviewed, it was argued. A means by which the distributor looked after the producer's interests as well as his own was thought desirable. But none of these ideas provided an answer to the NFFC's problems.

In 1957 its charter had been renewed for a further ten years under the Cinematograph Films Act with a capital of £6 million, plus £2 million on a Treasury guarantee. In the same year the British Film Fund Agency (formerly the British Film Production Fund or Eady Levy) became a statutory body and was also extended for ten years. Since 1950 it had raised a total of only £18 million, below the annual target figure of £3.5 million (ibid., p. 260). Both extensions indicated a recognition of the need for the continuation of a subsidy, although the Eady Levy was a redistribution of funds rather than a call on the public purse.

The NFFC made a profit of £50,000 in 1960 and provided finance for half the films shot in Britain, yet the almost inevitable pattern of losses was to resume during the 1960s. But the NFFC did fulfil a purpose and without it, as John Davis remarked, 'there would have been a complete financial collapse of British production' (Financial Times Annual Review of Industry 1954).

At the end of the decade, British studios were busier than they had been for some years. Not only were features being produced but short films and series for television. The British 'new wave', including such films as *Room at the Top* and *Saturday Night and Sunday Morning*, were box-office as well as critical successes. However, as John Spraos warned, there was a direct link between the rate of cinema closures and film production. British output had held up well in the 1950s, helped by 'expatriate' American films, but further closures and the continued ascendancy of Rank and ABC (with fewer cinemas on the third 'circuit') could hit production (Spraos, 1962, p. 133). British films do, he pointed out, obtain two-thirds of their earnings from the home market via exhibition and the Eady Levy; and without a circuit release, no British film could hope to meet its costs, let alone make a profit. The problem was to become more acute in succeeding years.

CHAPTER 7

Intermission

In the preceding chapters we outlined the various crises that have afflicted the British film industry since the end of the First World War. They included the drastic fall in production during the 1920s, which meant that by 1926 only 5% of the films shown in our cinemas were British. This situation resulted in the 1927 Cinematograph Films Act, which introduced a quota system to help, or protect, film-makers; but the speculative production boom of the early to mid 1930s was followed by a severe slump at the end of the decade. When war broke out in 1939 there were fears that the government would close down production altogether. In the post-war era, the 1947 sterling crisis led to an *ad valorem* duty on Hollywood films, a measure that provoked an embargo by US producers and the virtual closure of the North American market to British films. The 'opportunity' that the government believed had been given to British film-makers proved illusory, and the problems experienced by Rank in the late 1940s can be attributed, at least in part, to the imposition of the duty. By the mid 1950s the growing popularity of television was responsible for a dramatic decline in cinema attendances, which hit the exhibitors. Essentially, though, it has been British producers who have experienced the crises and government action has invariably focused on this branch of the industry.

Until the 1950s, the exhibitors built their circuits, struggled with the distributors over hire terms and suffered from the refusal of successive governments to make meaningful changes to the 'temporary' entertainments tax. But they prospered; many floated on the stock market, enjoying share ratings that reflected steady earnings and dividend growth as well as solid underlying assets.

The 1920s saw the beginning of the domination of the distribution trade by American companies who established offices in London and sold Hollywood films to British exhibitors. It was a relatively easy task, given the taste for their films that had developed during the 1914–18 war. The exhibitors were happy to rent what they knew audiences would pay to see, even if they resented the practices of blind and block booking.

Gradually, as the trend towards vertical integration gathered pace, important British distributors emerged, such as GFD, but the US 'majors' continued to handle the majority of the films on offer. Both the distributors and the exhibitors were involved in continual disputes with British producers over the quality of their films: the former were reluctant to handle 'inferior' material and the latter did not want to book films that would take a pittance at the box office.

In the early years of the century, British film-makers had supplied both the home and the overseas market. But even before the 1914–18 war began, production finance was not keeping pace with the growth of the cinema in Britain. Institutional investors, primarily based in the City of London, were wary of this aspect of the industry – a wariness that persists to this day – whereas Wall Street recognised the potential, and between 1914 and 1917 Hollywood gained an advantage that has never been lost. When the war ended there was no change in the attitude of British investors, and producers were unable to improve the overall quality of their films as a means of competing with Hollywood. There was no demand for their films in North American cinemas and the domestic market was not large enough to support British production.

The lack of capital has always dogged the British producer and without it few successful films can be made, either from a commercial or an artistic viewpoint. The independent producer, in particular, faced problems with distributors and exhibitors. Initially, he had to satisfy a distributor that his film would be popular with a mass audience – a necessity, since a distributor's guarantee was invariably needed to raise production finance. The distributor would negotiate the best terms possible from the exhibitor who had to take a mix of good, bad and indifferent films. If the proposed film was experimental or contained unusual subject matter, the inherently conservative distributors and exhibitors would be even more difficult to convince of its box-office appeal. Then as now, they have preferred to 'play safe', backing 'formula' pictures that have been successful with audiences, and Hollywood has always excelled at this kind of film. Although American examples predominate, British producers have had their successes; one thinks of the Gainsborough melo-dramas of the 1940s, the *Doctor in the House* series and the Norman Wisdom comedies in the 1950s, the *Carry On* films which began in 1958 and *James Bond* from the 1960s onwards.

In the period we have considered so far, the independent producer relied on loans, backed by a distribution guarantee, to fund the costs of his film, whereas the combines generally financed their produc-tions from internal resources. By the 1950s, however, Rank and ABPC had cut back on production and changed the methods by which they funded their films. In the financial year 1949–50, Rank wholly financed only 10 of the 20 films that the company made. The remain-ing 10 were financed jointly or via distribution agreements. In the same period, ABPC produced 11 films, funding six itself, with Warner Brothers paying for two others and the NFFC putting up some of the money for three (PEP 1952, pp. 251–52). Both combines were to finance the total costs of even fewer films in the following year.

Although a number of production companies had links with dis-tributors, this did not automatically ensure that capital would be available, and the 'independent' would need to raise the bulk of his costs by way of a short-term bank loan. He would also have to put up a percentage of the money himself. The illustration used in the PEP report showed a hypothetical feature film budget of £150,000 (a realistic figure for the time) and the breakdown was as follows (ibid., pp. 253–55):

	£	£
Own money	5,000	
Bank loan (front money)	105,000	
NFFC loan (front part of end money)	**40,000**	
		150,000
Completion money		10,000
		160,000*

* It was assumed that the production would cost more than the original budget

Own money is self-explanatory, but the bank loan could only be obtained on the basis of a distributor's guarantee (the return of an agreed percentage of the film's cost within, say, a year of its release; in this case 70% of the budget). Once the loan was forthcoming, the interest was deducted from the capital. The loan represented the front money and was the first charge on the producer's receipts.

The end money – the balance of the capital required – usually took the form of a loan, or loans, and in the PEP example it is assumed that the NFFC provided the money. The producer also needed a guarantor of completion, for without a finished film, the distributor's guarantee did not apply. In the early 1950s the fee charged was either 4% of the budget or 10% of the actual guarantee, and this was paid whether the film was completed or not. The last financial responsibility of the producer was to arrange insurance cover on all aspects of the production.

The various finance charges were allowed for in the original budget, and in the above example they amounted to £17,500, just under 12% of £150,000, a normal percentage for independent productions in the early 1950s. The sum was made up of bank loan £4,000, NFFC loan £3,000, guarantor of completion £6,000 and insurance £4,500.

Writing in 1955, Roger Manvell pointed out that to bring its producers £200,000 a film must take approximately six times that sum at the box office to allow for entertainments tax, the exhibitor's profits and expenses and the distributor's fee for handling the film (Manvell 1955, p. 187). He went on to give a breakdown of how box-office receipts were divided in percentage terms (ibid., p. 209):

Entertainments tax	35.4%
Exhibitor's share	41.6%
Distribution	7.1%
Newsreel hire	2.1%
Producer's share	13.8%

If a film recovered its costs and actually made a profit, it was likely that around 50% would be divided between the 'end money' providers (who bore the greatest risk), the distributor, and sometimes the guarantor of completion. If actors and others had agreed lower fees in exchange for a share of the profits, they would also benefit.

British producers were often accused of extravagance and there were many examples of budget overspending, but the post-war situation led to lower costs of production and much of the 'waste' that had been identified by industry observers was eliminated. The difficulty remained that a film needed high production values to succeed at the box office and this involved considerable expense. Cheap films looked cheap and failed as a result. After 1945 the industry as a whole suffered from the underemployment of its resources, and studio space was rarely fully occupied (around 60% at the beginning of the 1950s). Consequently, unemployment was high in the main union, the Association of Cine Technicians (ACT), and the uncertainty of employment led to higher rates of pay. The producer had to allow for this in his budget, and it was an important factor since some 80% of that budget was imputable to direct labour costs.

As the 1950s progressed, British production did improve, albeit marginally. From 1951 to 1956 the British Film Production Fund contributed an average of £2.6 million per year; 1952 was the peak year with £2.9 million (PEP 1958, p. 167). In addition to these sums, British producers received an average of £6.86 million per year in film hire during the same period; the peak was £7.8 million in 1954 (ibid., p. 167). The Eady Plan had put British production 'within reach of solvency' (PEP 1952, p. 293). Towards the end of the decade, the growing demand for TV films meant that producers had a new market; but unfortunately their traditional one, the cinema, was experiencing a sharp decline in attendances. This was more significant in terms of future profitability.

Britain has always had an abundance of film-making talent and our best films stand comparison with any that have been made abroad, but the British producer had to overcome many handicaps. The home market was not large enough for him to secure a reasonable return, or at least recoup his costs, on the majority of films that he made; and the difficulties of obtaining distribution in the North American market have been discussed in the first part of this survey. Given the costs of production, a film must be shown as widely as possible to have any chance of commercial success.

The absence of adequate funding was a perennial problem. Apart from isolated occasions, e.g. the flurry of activity before and after the 1927 Quota Act, investors avoided production companies while being prepared to put capital into the exhibition groups. They believed, usually correctly, that the risk outweighed the potential reward, and this very lack of investment resulted in producers being unable to make the more expensive films that were required to compete in world markets.

The control exercised by Hollywood through the popularity of its films and the strength of its distribution network made Britain, in effect, an extension of the US market. This 'colonisation' by Hollywood was criticised on cultural as well as economic grounds while the First World War was being fought and it certainly influenced subsequent government action to help the industry. That action took the form of protectionism, guaranteeing British films screen time in British cinemas with the underlying hope that a number of those films would earn American dollars. But, as we have seen, the quota system did not provide the springboard for a well-funded production industry that was able to match its Hollywood competitors. The post-war creation of the NFFC and the introduction of the Eady Levy were positive measures to help producers; they also underlined the fact that direct financial assistance from government was necessary if British film production was to be sustained. It was not, however, an idea that found favour with later administrations.

An early cinema: Lewisham Electric Palace c. 1910
Reproduced by permission of Lewisham Local Studies and Archives

Deutsch's vision, 'brand selling.' Odeon Well Hall, 1936

The original Gainsborough Studios, 1920s

Kind Hearts and Coronets, 1949
Reproduced by permission of Canal+ Image UK

Filming on the set of *Billy Liar*, 1963
Reproduced by permission of Canal+ Image UK

The Servant, 1964
Reproduced by permission of Canal+ Image UK

CHAPTER 8

The 1960s

THE INDUSTRY

Commentators in the mid 1960s described the British film industry as being in crisis, echoing what was happening in Italy and France. Declining audiences and cinema closures, the oversupply of films and limited circuit releases, the threat of television, all contributed to investor reluctance to finance films.

In 1960 there were 3,819 cinemas and admissions had fallen 10% from the previous year to 475 million. Gross takings were estimated at £62.5 million, 4% lower than in 1959. By 1969 there were only 1,581 cinemas, and total admissions had fallen to 215 million. Even allowing for inflation, gross takings had fallen to £58 million. (*Kine and TV Year Books* 1961 and 1971). ABC and Rank owned 226 and 256 cinemas respectively. By the late 1960s the Eady Levy was collecting between £4.2 million and £4.6 million each year, and without it, the British film production industry might have collapsed altogether, overwhelmed by the power of the Hollywood studios.

The growing popularity of television was a major cause of the decline in cinema audiences, leading to a vicious circle of cinema closures and a drop in admissions. John Spraos (1962) concluded that as many as 100 million visits a year were lost merely as a result of cinema closures by Rank and ABC. The consequences for British producers and distributors were catastrophic. In 1946 Britain had the highest per capita rate of cinema-going of the western world, with annual admissions of some 1.6 billion. (By 1984 that figure had collapsed to just 54 million.)

Faced by such a rapid decline in audiences, the Rank and ABC duopoly was not prepared at that time to invest in either cinema or films. This lack of investment in film was echoed by another purchasing duopoly, this time in television. The BBC and ITV, as the only two television networks, kept the value of television rights low.

It would be easy to conclude that the film industry declined in the 1960s and 1970s mainly because of the influence of television. Smaller cinema audiences led to inevitable cinema closures, with many local cinemas being converted to bingo halls. Fewer cinema screens also meant a smaller distribution channel for feature films and so demand was undermined. But there were other causes.

It did not help that so much of British cinema at the time was parochial. Many films were produced for English audiences with its own humour and customs, which did not always translate well into other languages. There were notable exceptions like David Lean's *Lawrence of Arabia*.

As the television companies prospered, they acquired some of the old film studios such as Teddington. Directors and writers moved to television instead of cinema, and directors like Ken Russell and John Schlesinger started their careers in television and only later moved to the big screen. Later this trend moved to directors making their name in producing commercials and then moving to television and cinema.

American finance for British films accelerated in the 1960s, and their productions in the UK to a large extent saved the industry. A combination of antitrust legislation in the US breaking the majors' control of distribution and the strength of the mighty dollar conspired to make overseas investment attractive for Hollywood studios. For a Hollywood producer, savings of up to 30% could be made by filming in the UK. The Eady Levy was an added attraction as this gave a subsidy for a film registered as British, even where the finance came from abroad.

The technical talent in Britain was cheaper, and with good studios and popular British films, US investment grew, reaching a peak in 1968 of £31.3 million invested in British subsidiaries of US majors. The previous year 90% of production finance was American, coming from companies like United Artists, Paramount, Warner Brothers, MGM, Twentieth Century–Fox, Columbia, Universal and Disney.

So this was the decade when American money flooded into Britain, assisted by the strong dollar and Eady money. As the costs of producing films in Hollywood rose, American films were produced in Britain, Italy and France. This traffic came to be known as 'runaway production' with productions being made more cheaply and with far fewer problems from the trade unions compared to Hollywood.

Another trend between 1955 and 1965 was that co-productions of all films made in Europe increased from 10% to 40%, including classic French-Italian co-productions such as *The Leopard* and *Belle de Jour*. But Britain did not share in this. Insulated by the Eady Levy, American films being made in English studios, and the difficulty of foreign languages, independent producers deliberately failed to grasp the opportunities for co-productions.

DISTRIBUTION AND EXHIBITION

The decade started with 26% of British cinemas being controlled by the Rank and ABC circuits. Adjusting for the size and location of cinemas measured by seating capacity, by 1963 the two companies controlled 41.5% of cinema seats, and in London this domination yielded handsome profits as the London area accounted for more than a quarter of the national box-office takings (*Sight & Sound*, Autumn 1963).

The Rank Organisation in 1961 estimated that an average return to the distributors would be about £90,000 from Rank release, £80,000 from ABC release and only £35,000—40,000 from third circuit release. Inevitably, distributors preferred to join the queue for time on a major circuit for general release rather than be sidelined on the third circuit.

The dilemma for distributors was increased by the gap between the earnings of the few very successful films and the rest. To screen commercially viable films, Rank and ABC could negotiate from a position of strength and the smaller independent cinema chain from weakness. The consequences for film producers were serious. If the distributor was denied a circuit release, then the film would never make money.

The domination of the Rank and Associated British Picture Corporation (ABPC) duopoly continued throughout the decade until

1969 when ABPC was absorbed by EMI, which was later to become Thorn-EMI Screen Entertainment.

In early 1967 the Monopolies and Mergers Commission published a report on the film industry. Its findings were unequivocal and damning: 'More than one-third by value ... of the films supplied to exhibitors in Great Britain are supplied to companies within the Rank Organisation' (*Sight & Sound*, Winter 1966/67). Rank and ABC 'so conducted their respective affairs as to restrict competition in connection with the supply of films.' Trade 'barring' practices 'restrict the freedom of distributors to offer films to other exhibitors.' The report concluded that various trade practices operate against the public interest, placing barriers on freedom of choice of films.

By the mid 1960s, the number of cinemas in Britain had fallen below 2,000. Rank and ABC controlled some 600, which included nearly three-quarters of the country's 400 largest cinemas: 1,500 seats or more. With the aim of screening commercial films, independent film producers and distributors faced three problems. First, too many cinemas were too big to be a practicable venue for more experimental films that would give the public a wider choice. Secondly, because the smaller cinemas could not compete for successful films, they lacked the finance to offer a good selection of popular films. Thirdly, a two-tier class system of films and cinemas became a self-fulfilling prophesy.

The commission recommended a more free and flexible market, with certain trade practices to be curtailed, and leaving it to Rank and ABC to give 'limited ... circuit bookings to films of limited appeal.' It did not consider that the third circuit possessed either the finance, the films or the audiences to make it work.

In commenting on the commission's findings, the *Financial Times* said: 'the whole history of Government relations with the film industry suggests strongly that a rigid line should be drawn between subsidising art and subsidising commercial inefficiency.'

Rank and ABC circuits between them could take only 104 first features a year (making no allowance for double bills), and a circuit release was vital for a producer to stand a chance to recover his costs. These two circuits allocated general release dates, sharing them between their own features and those produced by independents. In 1963 Rank screened 23 British first features (10 being their own release) and 27 foreign films, and ABC screened 26 British first features, 14 of them from their own distribution company, Warner-Pathé, and 24 foreign films. So the typical release pattern that year was for 50% British films, against a basic quota obligation of 30% (*Sight & Sound*, Winter 1963).

Despite what appears to be a reasonable statistic, producers complained of having to wait for up to one year for a circuit screening, with all the inevitable adverse financial and promotional implications.

Unless the Rank or ABC circuit was secured by a distributor, a British first feature film stood no chance of recovering its costs. The film bookers at each of these circuits were immensely influential. The Federation of British Film Makers, in its submission to the Cinematograph Films Council, suggested that, *for booking purposes only*, the circuits should be fragmented, with no one man booking for more than 25 cinemas. Many in the industry felt that the dominance of the duopoly and its control over which films were screened served as a barrier to independent producers raising film finance. This was especially galling when films produced by the majors flopped at the box office, taking up valuable screen time.

The Federation of Film Unions proposed resurrecting the third release to have the same booking and revenue power as Rank and ABC. But with increasing cinema closures, where would the screens come from? The Federation of British Film Makers, representing most of the independents, wanted to increase the quota from 30% to 50%. Some even proposed splitting cinema ownership from film production, which could only be achieved by legislation, which the Labour government was not minded to do.

So the independents were still dependent on Rank and ABC for circuit release. Then in December 1968, EMI who already controlled 25% of its equity, launched a £34 million bid for the balance of the shares of Associated British Picture Corporation. The commercial logic was to combine EMI's recording, electronic and Grade Organisation interests with ABPC's chain of 270 ABC cinemas, film production, bowling alleys and its Thames TV stake, creating one of the world's largest entertainment groups. The bid was increased one month later to £41 million and EMI strengthened its hold on British cinema.

IMPACT OF TELEVISION

America led the way with television, a threat the Hollywood studios initially very much feared, so much so that they refused to allow the networks access to their film libraries. But after the first network broadcast of MGM's *The Wizard of Oz* in November 1956 on CBS, which attracted 40 million viewers, the studios belatedly realised that television could give them a new stream of income from their film libraries, and from 1960 the revenue from selling television rights cushioned the studios' losses from declining cinema audiences. The studios could do this because, being vertically integrated and controlling both film production and distribution, they still owned the copyright to their film libraries, and so could exploit the new television rights.

This realisation was slower in Britain, partly because the market penetration of television in homes took longer, and partly because there was a fundamental suspicion about the impact of television on the cinema. As far back as 1935, a year before the BBC broadcast television, two British film trade associations banned their members from selling television rights.

In 1958 the Film Industry Defence Organisation (FIDO) was formed in response to Ealing Studios' plans to sell a hundred films to television. Funded by a modest levy on box-office receipts, FIDO paid film-makers a nominal sum to sign a covenant binding them not to sell their films to television. Unsurprisingly, the duopoly of Rank and Associated British Picture Corporation were vocal supporters of FIDO. Surprisingly, Sidney Bernstein of Granada, a company operating a chain of cinemas and one of Britain's first commercial television stations, also supported FIDO because he believed television viewers would be satisfied with live programming and original drama.

Producers refusing to sign the covenant faced a boycott from the exhibitors, resulting in their films not being screened. Lew Grade's Associated Television bought a package of fifty movies from Samuel Goldwyn, who was immediately black-listed. As late as 1963, defiant cinema-owners were still insisting that 'FIDO has been the envy of the world' (Jackson 1980). Some films would remain on FIDO's list for decades because the covenant lasted as long as the copyright existed in the film.

But by the mid 1960s FIDO collapsed mainly because American independent producers were desperate for cash. US cinema audiences had fallen 82% in just twenty years. The opportunity for selling television rights in Britain and refusing to sign the FIDO covenant had become an economic necessity.

A vicious circle had formed. The growth in television led to declining audiences, which led to cinema closures: the fall in admissions resulted in lower revenues for producers, which led to a fall in production. As many independent producers had already pre-sold the rights to distributors to finance the production of the film, they could not exploit the television rights, and anyway, the film industry only had itself to blame for being so slow off the mark in exploiting television.

It did not help that the BBC and ITV were both sufficiently well funded that they did not need to create production partnerships with film producers. They could buy their extra programming cheaply from the Americans, which is why programmes like *I Love Lucy* came to Britain. Television was also developing its own distribution and financing programmes. The 1960s saw the beginning of television production at Pinewood. Lew Grade, managing director of Associated Television, financed Gerry Anderson's *Thunderbirds* and his other productions. Grade had his own distribution company, Incorporated Television Company (ITC).

FILM FINANCE

By 1967 it was estimated that as much as 90% of funding for films made in the UK came from America, and the term 'Hollywood, England' was heard. United Artists was very active, financing films including the Beatles' *A Hard Day's Night* and the *James Bond* films produced by Albert 'Cubby' Broccoli, who with Harry Saltzman had formed EON Productions.

One hundred and sixty films were made at Pinewood during this decade, including *Whistle Down the Wind*, produced by Richard Attenborough and directed by Bryan Forbes, *Those Magnificent Men in their Flying Machines* made by Twentieth Century—Fox, *The Ipcress File* with Michael Caine, and *Chitty Chitty Bang Bang*. Charles

Chaplin returned to England in 1966 to direct *The Countess from Hong Kong* starring Sophia Loren and Marlon Brando, and Ronald Neame directed *The Prime of Miss Jean Brodie*. But by the end of the decade American investment disappeared after expensive flops, including *The Battle of Britain* and *Goodbye, Mr Chips*, and the losses being made by Hollywood studios. British producers were again facing a serious funding crisis.

While the state of the British film industry from the independent producers' perspective was parlous, the studios like Pinewood, Elstree and Shepperton and the post-production houses in London were enjoying a boom. International productions backed by American money, which tapped into Eady money, were coming to London. But what was attracting directors like Truffaut, Kubrick, Chaplin, and Dick Lester?

Leaving aside the appeal of 'swinging sixties' London, American studios were being attracted by the investment climate for films in Europe, and especially London. MGM was financing Kubrick and Antonioni, MCA was funding Truffaut, and Fox was backing Joe Losey. British crews were making the films, which meant they qualified for quota and Eady money.

The size of foreign investment in the British film industry was huge. Andrew Filson, director of the Federation of British Film Makers, declared in the spring of 1966 that 85% of British film-making in that year will be American financed. 'Two-thirds of the 69 feature length films made in England in 1965 were 100% American financed' (*Sight & Sound*, Spring 1966).

So British film producers were being financed by dollars, which gave them access to world markets and the chance of 100% finance rather than chasing after 'front' and 'end' money and relying on deficit financing. Lord Birkett was speaking for the industry when he said in a House of Lords debate, 'Until there is a solid and competitive alternative in British finance, film-makers in Britain would view with the greatest alarm anything which would deter the Americans' (Houston 1963). Lord Archibald added that the problem was not one of American investment, rather it was the lack of British investment in its own film industry.

To attract investment into film-making and to attract British film-makers into getting finance from British sources, that is the conundrum the NFFC was trying to solve with its inadequate resources. The other major source of assistance to British film-makers was Eady money at an annual limit of £5 million. This scheme, devised to help British film-makers, increasingly served as an extra incentive for the Americans to film in the UK. Because Eady money was calculated on box-office returns, the American-backed *Goldfinger* and *Tom Jones* were each subsidised by a million dollars, and *Variety* estimated that *Thunderball* received $2.1 million from the fund, which at the existing exchange rate represented nearly 15% of the fund's total annual revenue.

Eady money was designed to be a form of self-help, originally accepted voluntarily by the industry and only later made statutory. It was subsidising successful films at the expense of less commercial films that struggled to raise funding, and with 80% of British films losing money at the box office, the British film industry was in serious decline. While other European countries provided elaborate systems of subsidies to their domestic film industries, British policy was to leave its film industry to fend for itself.

As the journalist Penelope Houston wrote, 'It sometimes seems that a kind of madness is needed to invest in British film production at all (*British* British films that is, as opposed to the American British variety), like someone at a roulette table obstinately and fatalistically backing zero on every spin' (*Sight & Sound*, Spring 1966).

British Lion was typical of the British film studios at this time. At the beginning of the 1960s its fortunes were boosted by the number of American productions that were filmed at its Shepperton studios. The Eady Levy, the generally low costs of production and the plentiful supply of creative and technical talent created a boom that lasted until the end of the decade. Between 1960 and 1970 it has been estimated that over 90% of the capital invested in film production was American money (Threadgall 1994).

This trend started in the 1950s, and in 1961 British Lion entered into a distribution agreement with Columbia Pictures that cemented their relationship and led to films such as *The Guns of Navarone* (1961), David Lean's *Lawrence of Arabia* (1962), *Doctor No* (1962), and *A Man for All Seasons* (1966) being made at Shepperton. The studios were also used by independent producers who were increasingly producing series for television such as *Danger Man*.

In their financial year 1961–62, British Lion received what was in effect a cash injection of over £300,000 from FIDO (as payment for the television rights to its films) and profits leapt to £576,800. The next year, albeit on more modest profits of £119,225, the payment of a 5% ordinary dividend was announced, the first since 1957.

In 1963 the share capital of the company was restructured and the NFFC's original shareholding of 600,000 deferred shares was replaced by 300,000 ordinary shares plus cash of £591,000. The NFFC was entitled to buy the remaining 50% of the shares that it did not already own from the directors. They exercised their option the following year, which valued British Lion at £1.59 million, and this was the amount paid to the NFFC when British Lion was sold to a consortium headed by Sir Michael Balcon in March 1964.

Doubts about the future of British Lion hit profitability during this time, but by 1966–67 profits had recovered strongly to £198,796, helped by the box-office success of *Casino Royale* and *A Man for All Seasons*. However, expenditure in studio improvements and a downturn in the next financial year required a new capital injection. In order to raise much needed finance, Hambros Bank sponsored a stock market flotation in 1968 when over 1 million new shares were issued at a price of 16s 6d. But the higher profile did not help earnings: in 1968–69 and 1969–70 profits fell to £63,334 and £46,848 respectively. By now the American producers were cutting back and Shepperton, together with other British studios, suffered the consequences.

In an interesting postscript, Sidney Gilliat, British Lion's chairman, later recalled an event which not only flagged the impending downturn for British Lion, but also revealed a telling insight into the role and attitude of the banks at that time. In 1993 he recalled:

Somewhere between 1966 and 1969, when our principal bankers at British Lion were the National Provincial Bank (later merged with the Westminster Bank into today's National Westminster Bank), who advanced the loans for almost every picture made under the aegis of British Lion, a cocktail party was held at the Bank's Green Street, Mayfair branch. ... I got into a conversation with a Bank official who confided that things were going to be much more difficult for us all in the future. He indicated very firmly that the bank was going to take a much harder look at the financing of films, since a producer had actually defaulted on an outstanding loan. I realised from what the official had said that the Bank actually thought that *all* films paid their loans back wholly out of film revenues. Of course, the policy at British Lion and elsewhere was to repay loans the normal eighteen months after release and British Lion, like everybody else in an *overall* solvent position, had duly repaid every loan after eighteen months out of their resources whether the picture concerned was profitable by then or not. If our bank official was right, therefore, the Bank must have been living for years under the delusion that *all* films got their loans back from revenue. When they examined the defaulting production company, it appears to have dawned on them that National Provincial Bank-financed films were not all profitable. The man finished our conversation by saying: 'I'm very sorry, but all you fellows, as a result, are going to find film funding from us much more difficult.' Not long after this event, National Provincial virtually ceased to finance new films altogether.

After that date, financing of films became increasingly much more difficult. For instance, if I remember rightly, the last two films made under the old British Lion ... were financed by a consortium, the bank involved being the Bank of America. It may seem strange that one man's default on a single picture should have set alarm bells ringing to such an uncalled for extent, but I have always regarded financial bodies as possessing at least as much uninformed innocence as keen eyes acumen. (Threadgall 1994, pp. 113–14)

CHAPTER 9

The 1970s

THE INDUSTRY

The early 1970s witnessed a continuing decline in cinema attendances, cutbacks and closures of the UK production arms of the Hollywood studios, the reduction in British government subsidies to the National Film Finance Corporation (NFFC), and the declining profitability of the few independent production companies then based in Britain (Eberts and Ilott 1992).

The American economy and Hollywood were in recession, and American studios were pulling out of British production. Hollywood was in crisis in the early 1970s with five of the seven major studios making losses. The trend of American investment in British films was waning, and since the peak in 1968, US companies invested just £2.9 million in 1974. The oil crisis, economic recession and huge losses from failed big-budget films were hitting home, and the impact was felt by independent producers in the UK. In 1971 there were 98 registered British films. By 1976 this had dropped to 70 and the number was falling.

So the decade started with the fortunes of the British film industry at a low ebb. The twin pillars of government aid via the NFFC and Hollywood studios cash that had sustained the industry for the last twenty years suddenly collapsed, leaving independent film producers high and dry.

During a debate in the House of Commons in the spring of 1970 for new legislation on the film industry, Mrs Gwyneth Dunwoody MP, a parliamentary secretary to the Board of Trade said, 'Ever since I have been in the Board of Trade it seems to me that we have done nothing but review the film industry. This is a difficult industry' (Houston 1970). Sir Keith Joseph, later to become a key adviser to Margaret Thatcher, remarked, 'Its financing is very strange' (Houston 1970). Other MPs added the adjectives curious, crazy and complicated.

Penelope Houston observed, 'It seems impossible for anyone to discuss the film industry without finding its ways exceptional and mysterious; and perhaps this makes for conservatism, and a reluctance to tamper in any way unnecessarily with the works' (Houston 1970).

The government Films Bill again settled for the status quo. There remained the triplet structure to support British film production – Quota, the British Film Fund (Eady money) and the NFFC. The NFFC's interest payments on bad investments were written off and it was given an additional £5 million government loan to serve as a 'bank of last resort', 'pump primer' or 'bridging operation' as it was variously described. Even the composition of the Cinematographic Films Council remained unchanged. The Labour government's explanation for the absence of change was given by Mrs Dunwoody. She had received so many conflicting suggestions from so many quarters of the film industry that their effect was to cancel each other out.

However, there were two minor but significant changes. The Film Fund should give a grant to the British Film Institute Production Board and also give money to pay for some of the running costs of the proposed National Film School. Cinema interests were inevitably opposed to extending the levy, and Sir Keith Joseph for the Tory opposition agreed with them, saying any additional money should come from the Department of Education and Science. Concerning the NFFC, the Tories' view that it should be phased out was based on the assumption that private capital from the City would be forthcoming, like Morgan Grenfell's de Grunwald programme. But as Mrs Dunwoody said in a parliamentary debate, 'The important part of the Bill, in many ways, is the refunding of the NFFC' (Houston 1970).

The number of cinemas in 1971 was 1,553 and many were only half-filled. The radical concept of 'twinning' started, whereby the cinema was divided into two smaller screens, or a complex of cinemas formed a unit like Cinecenta's multiple of four screens behind Leicester Square. The old cinemas were falling into decay and mini cinemas were springing up. There was no shortage of films, but most were from Hollywood and the Continent.

By 1972 Rank and EMI controlled 32% of the cinemas, which generated 52% of total takings (Economic Intelligence Unit 1972). In that year Lord Rank died. He had played a dominant role in saving the British film industry by creating a vertically integrated film company, combining production, exhibition and distribution. In the late 1940s and early 1950s his benevolence allowed film-makers creative and financial freedom. It was ironic that by the time he died, the Rank Organisation had forgotten its Methodist origins and followed corporate fashion to become a conglomerate, with business interests ranging from film, bingo, casinos and a highly successful investment in Rank Xerox copying machines. Its lack of investment in its cinemas made a night out for the public less than enticing.

The British film industry started restructuring with a series of takeovers in the early 1970s. Barclay Securities secured control of British Lion, putting the future of Shepperton Studios in doubt. Then J.H. Vavasseur offered to buy out the Barclay Securities group for £20 million to add further uncertainty to the studios. A golden period for British film production was suddenly and painfully at an end. City money was taking over from the creative and artistic interests, although there were some experienced film hands at Vavasseur.

But on the artistic front all was not lost. The liberal trend in censorship from the mid 1960s was continuing with increasing tolerance shown towards film producers. In 1971 the British Film Producers' Association annual report referred to co-production treaties with Canada and Australia, and Mrs Gwyneth Dunwoody was appointed as a director. She recognised the film industry was a difficult one. The government-sponsored National Film School was opened, directed by Professor Colin Young from the University of California, to train potential film-makers.

The NFFC's resources were dwindling, and between 1973 and 1981 it contributed only £4 million towards 31 features and 6 shorts. However, cinema audiences were returning, attracted by big disaster movies like *Earthquake* and *The Towering Inferno*. In 1974 there were 138 million admissions, a figure not to be seen again until the year 2000.

Recognising that to achieve international success meant attracting American audiences, the three British majors — EMI, Lord Grade's Associated Communications Corporation, and Rank — produced a series of blockbusters that all flopped, the biggest loser being Lord Grade's *Raise the Titanic* which ended up costing $35 million. Later Lord Grade commented ruefully, 'It would have been cheaper to lower the Atlantic' (Puttnam 1997, p. 307).

In 1979 Margaret Thatcher's Conservative Party came to power on a platform of deregulating markets and cutting taxes. In Geoffrey Howe's first Budget, the chancellor applied value added tax to cinema tickets and trimmed £0.5 million from the budget of the NFFC, whose future was already under review. The British Film Institute also found its budget being cut by 2% at a time when inflationary costs were increasing. On a positive note, the cut in personal taxes was anticipated to attract back British stars who had become tax exiles during the previous twenty years, stars including Rex Harrison, James Mason, David Niven, Michael Caine, Sean Connery and Roger Moore.

Against this economic and political background, raising film finance was becoming increasingly difficult. But by the end of the decade, new tax concessions in the form of capital allowances, and new distribution channels in the form of video, and cable and pay television in America were creating new markets for film. In Britain, directors like Ridley Scott, who had made his name directing television commercials, directed *Alien*, which was an immediate box-office hit.

Rank (Odeon cinemas) and EMI Films (ABC cinemas) dominated the UK market, both as distributors and producers, and so they could compete with the London branch offices of the Hollywood studios. (During this period, EMI produced films like *The Deer Hunter*, *Warlords of Atlantis*, *Death on the Nile* and *Convoy*.) So they would be a first port of call for any independent producer.

In the late 1970s, former venture capitalist Jake Eberts opened a small office in Mayfair and launched Goldcrest Films, a company which was to have a dramatic impact on the British film industry.

GOLDCREST

In 1978 *Watership Down* was released. Jake Eberts had pulled together $50,000 development finance and given those investors a tenfold return on their initial investment.

Eberts' vision was to concentrate on film development financing only. He would bridge the gap, taking a concept, packaging it and selling it on to investors to fund the film production, and receiving a carried interest in any profits from the film. It was a familiar practice in Hollywood. But selling a package rather than the film is more difficult; it requires a good track record and a good relationship with the distributor. As the distributor is taking a greater risk, his return will be that much higher as a consequence.

In January 1977, Goldcrest was launched as a new film development-finance company, backed by Roger Brooke of Pearson Longman and Michael Stoddart of Electra, a leading venture capital fund in the City. Goldcrest's subsidiary, Firecrest, was registered in the Channel Islands, which achieved certain tax benefits for overseas film projects. The concept was to provide development finance only, not to fund the production of films. That was to come later.

Pearson Longman's investment was £100,000 in the development fund, Goldcrest Films, in 1977. Eberts then drafted a prospectus to raise a minimum of £5 million, and from the beginning of 1979 to the middle of 1980 he approached more than 150 potential investors around the world. Finally he resorted to his existing backers, Pearson Longman, who invested half the $1 million which Goldcrest, via its subsidiary, Firecrest, invested in International Film Investors (IFI) in 1978. IFI was a $10 million fund sponsored by E.F. Hutton. To a company the size of Pearson Longman, these were not significant sums.

Putting the film package together by securing the film rights, developing the script (and storyboard if it was an animation), selecting a director and principal actors, creating the budget, and finding production finance from third parties, Goldcrest's objective was to build a portfolio of film-makers and films. It was not in the early years of its corporate life in the business of producing or financing films – it focused entirely on development, recouping its investment when the film was made.

On the basis that major studios convert about 1 project in 20, a good independent development financier might expect to convert 3 or 4 in 10. Goldcrest was aiming higher, because it was going to work exclusively with established film-makers which made it easier to raise production finance. In the first two years, Goldcrest provided development finance for five films, *Black Jack*, *Breaking Glass*, *Chariots of Fire*, *The Plague Dogs* and *Enigma*.

COMMERCIAL TELEVISION

The 1970s saw the start of the golden age for television commercials, which became a training ground for some of the most successful British film directors of the future. Directors like David Puttnam, Alan Parker, Hugh Hudson, and Ridley Scott all started their careers in advertising.

Ridley Scott, who has produced more than 3,000 television commercials since the 1970s and went on to direct blockbusters including *Blade Runner*, *Alien*, *Thelma and Louise*, *Hannibal* and *Gladiator*, became the most successful British director in box-office terms. His work won acclaim from the business world, and perhaps his most notable commercials were the nostalgic series for Hovis bread. He views commercials as 'mini-films', providing a director with the discipline and stamina to produce quality work quickly.

Producers willingly embraced the potential of television as another distribution channel for their films. Exploiting the copyright of a film now included planning a distribution schedule, which included cinema exhibition, television and cable sales, and video and rental sales.

Lord Grade was emerging as a potential third force by the end of the decade. In early 1979 Associated Communications Corporation, a film production and distribution group, paid £12.5 million for Laurie Marsh's Intereuropean group, which owned the Classic cinema chain. The deal challenged the duopoloy of EMI and Rank, as this deal created a vertically integrated group, combining exhibition with production and distribution.

The Classic cinema chain included 141 screens in 81 locations and a valuable site off Piccadilly. This compared to EMI's 308 screens on 156 sites and Rank's 272 screens on 142 sites (*Screen International*, February 1979).

Lord Grade was also expanding into Europe, and he was predicting a $100 million gross from *The Muppet Movie*. His Black Lion subsidiary planned making a minimum of five British films a year for the

British market at budgets between 1 and 2 million dollars, and by the summer of 1979 *Raise the Titanic* was going into production. But this film and *On Golden Pond* was to push his company to the verge of bankruptcy.

FILM FINANCE

The government's introduction of the capital tax allowance scheme proved to be a catalyst for the British film industry. It would be a major setback when in April 1985 capital allowances were phased out. Tax shelter finance was available in the 1970s in the form of complex sale and leaseback arrangements. But these schemes attracted investors who were more interested in the tax break than the investment, and the schemes were designed to benefit the investor more than the film producer. Morgan Grenfell launched a film production fund in 1971, but just two years later the entire fund was lost.

FILM STUDIOS

The film studios like Pinewood were increasingly being used by television to produce series like *The New Avengers, The Persuaders* and *Space 1999*. One hundred and twenty-five films were made at Pinewood during the 1970s, and visiting Hollywood directors included Billy Wilder for *The Private Life of Sherlock Holmes* and Alfred Hitchcock for *Frenzy.*

In 1976 Pinewood built the world's largest sound stage and investment was made in equipment for television and video production. The economics of the studios was changing. Previously, a studio needed to make 20 films a year to make a profit, but now with the big blockbusters requiring special effects, it took only two blockbusters like *Superman I* and *Superman II* to keep the studio fully occupied.

Despite declining American investment in British films in the 1970s, studios like Pinewood still offered a cost-effective venue for Paramount's production of *The Great Gatsby*. In addition to the *Bond* and *Carry On* films, other productions of the decade included *Fiddler on the Roof,* Alan Parker's film debut *Bugsy Malone,* and Agatha Christie's murder mystery *Death on the Nile* with an all-star cast.

By the early 1970s fewer films were being made at Shepperton Studios and the financial year 1971–72 showed net losses of £1.2 million (against a profit in the previous year of £143,000). An exceptional write-off of £805,000 on British Lion films was the main reason for the sharp downturn. However, the studios were valued at £1.728 million in the balance sheet and were certainly worth more; and this factor lay behind the bid from John Bentley's Barclay Securities in early 1972.

British Lion had already been in merger talks with the Star Group, and when the discussions collapsed, Bentley stepped in with an offer of £5.5 million. The approach was supported by British Lion's bankers, and the bid went through in April 1972. In fact, only 60% of the shareholders accepted and Bentley gained control at a cost of around £3 million in cash and shares.

John Bentley had the reputation of being an asset-stripper and Barclay Securities had been built on a series of audacious acquisitions. He was attracted by the potential value of redeveloping a 60 acre site at Shepperton Studios with the core businesses of British Lion – a distribution company, film library, and Pearl & Dean – in the price for almost nothing. Bentley estimated that the total assets were worth some £20 million (Threadgall 1994, p. 122). That the studios were loss-making supported Bentley's view that they should be closed and the site used for a possible housing development.

The planned closure of Shepperton provoked a strong response. An action committee was formed, backed by local residents and the film unions. The NFFC still held one preference share in British Lion which, among other rights, gave it the power to veto any disposal of the 'interests' of Shepperton Studios. This, combined with the success of the action committee, frustrated Bentley's plans in the following months and in November 1972 a new public company, Lion International, was floated on behalf of Barclay Securities. Its assets comprised British Lion Films, Shepperton Studios and Pearl & Dean.

It now began to look likely that an agreement, or at least a compromise, would be reached with 40 acres of land being sold for development and 20 acres retained as a studio complex. Although John Bentley had been backed into a corner and accepted the proposal, in March 1973 Barclay Securities was taken over by J.H. Vavasseur Ltd, the finance group. The question now was what Vavasseur would do regarding Shepperton. The answer came in November 1973 when it was agreed that eight stages would survive on a 22 acre site. The remaining acreage would be sold off for development.

But in the middle of a serious economic recession and stock market downturn, Vavasseur itself was in trouble. Confidence in the group was lost, especially in its insurance business, which led to a restructuring of the company by Hambros Bank. Vavasseur retained a controlling interest in Lion International who, ironically, saw trading profits jump by 34% to £2.5 million in the financial year 1973−74, despite losses at Shepperton of £469,000 (ibid., p. 139).

In 1975 only four films were produced at the 'new' Shepperton studios. Outline planning permission was given for housing on the 40 acre site, and in July the managing directors of British Lion Films, Barry Spikings and Michael Deeley, bought British Lion Ltd from Vavasseur for £1.2 million. Its independence was short-lived. EMI purchased the company for £730,000 with the blessing of the NFFC in 1976, and the NFFC sold its special preference share to British Lion.

Lion International had changed its name to Mills & Allen International, and that company still owned Shepperton Studios in 1975. Vavasseur, by this time rescued by the Bank of England's 'lifeboat', held 78.9% of Mills & Allen's equity. Both Mills & Allen and its majority shareholder began to show signs of recovery and managed the studios until they were acquired by Lee Electric (Lighting) Ltd in 1984.

Despite the turbulent background, a number of successful films were produced at Shepperton during the 1970s, including *The Day of the Jackal* (1972), *The Omen* (1975), and Ridley Scott's *Alien* (1978). Unfortunately, there were not enough productions to make Shepperton profitable and in 1979 only three films were made at the studios.

CHAPTER 10

The 1980s

If the trade papers of the day were to be believed, the early 1980s exuded a sense that the film business was over in England. But this was to be the nadir of its fortunes, because the seeds for the resurgence of the British film industry started in this decade and flowered in the mid 1990s. By the early 1980s there were four television channels and two, BBC2 and Channel 4, were beginning to invest in films. Channel 4 led the way by producing films for both television and the cinema such as *My Beautiful Launderette*.

Margaret Thatcher's Tory government was against government subsidies for any industry and its entire ethos was for industries and individuals to stand on their own feet. Inevitably, film subsidies via the National Film Corporation and the Eady Levy, foundations of British film production since 1949, were abolished in 1985, leaving the industry to fend for itself as market forces ruled.

Cinema admissions fell to 54 million in 1984, the lowest since records began in 1933. A year later admissions started to rise as exhibitors began building multiplex cinemas, which gave audiences more choice, more comfortable surroundings and a higher quality of customer service. Audiences were also attracted back to wide-screens by the big epic films of directors like George Lucas (*Star Wars)* and Steven Spielberg (*Close Encounters of the Third Kind, ET*).

Goldcrest Films was seen as the new exciting face of the UK film industry, a platform for British creative and technical talent, until its failure in the late 1980s. Despite its collapse, Goldcrest's influence and legacy should never be underestimated. The company raised the profile of the industry and showed that UK producers could produce internationally successful films. A renaissance in the British film industry was beginning, albeit falteringly.

The major Hollywood studios also increased their output in the 1980s and a rising proportion of them used UK locations and post-production facilities. By the end of the decade, the Hollywood studios were grossing more than ever before on a series of adventure movies, but the ignominious end of Goldcrest left the renaissance in the independent film industry in ruins in terms of its financing and how British investors perceived film investment.

THE INDUSTRY

Against a background of falling cinema attendances and the advent of the home video camcorder, the Association of Independent Producers estimated that 97% of film watching was done outside cinemas. With television and an estimated 13 million people having access to videocassette players in their homes, some 4 million video films every week were being rented by 1983, in addition to film being copied from the TV networks. Attendances dropped disastrously during the 1980s when film-going was in the doldrums. But the industry fought back with multiplex cinemas offering more comfort and choice.

The new technologies of video and cable television were changing the structure of the film industry, cutting the supply chain between the film producer and the audience. So although the growth in television programmes in the 1960s and 1970s had led to a massive decline in cinema attendances, increasing video sales and rentals in the 1980s actually stimulated cinema attendances.

In 1981 the total number of registered British films was just 36. In that year the Tory government restructured the National Film Finance Corporation (NFFC) in partnership with the private sector. The government contributed £1 million to be matched by £5 million funding from the private sector. As a sweetener, the NFFC was also to receive proceeds from the Eady Levy, either £1.5 million or 20% of the levy's gross receipts, whichever was higher. The levy also contributed funds to the National Film and Television School and the British Film Institute (BFI) Production Board.

But the NFFC was to become discredited following its track record of backing a string of turkeys with what in effect were government loans, many of which were never repaid, and in 1985 Margeret Thatcher scrapped the NFFC.

The film industry was weak and felt that it had no government support. David Puttnam, who was to play an important role in Goldcrest, was scornful of the Tory government's lack of interest in film-making. Introducing a keynote report on the film industry at the time, he commented: 'In Nicholas Ridley, we've got a Secretary of State who gives the impression that he would regard [it as] his greatest success at the Department of Trade and Industry if he could close the British film industry down.'

British Film Year was a 1985 initiative to promote the film industry and revive cinema-going. Although actively supported by such luminaries as David Puttnam and Richard Attenborough, it met with indifference from the leading distributors in Wardour Street, the very companies who would benefit the most. Ironically, the trend was already reversing, and audiences were returning to see the big action movies being produced by Hollywood.

In 1986 Thorn-EMI Screen Entertainment, with its large cinema chain and EMI Films, was taken over by Cannon. So now only one of the powerful duopoly was British. By the end of the decade there were 1,561 screens in Britain: Cannon operated 381 of them on 138 sites and Rank's Odeon chain operated 256 screens on 75 sites (*BFI Handbook* 1991). According to Street (1997), both companies gave preferential screenings to films produced by their American affiliates, Columbia and Warner (Cannon), and Disney, Twentieth Century–Fox, United Artists and Universal (Rank).

By the late 1980s, the trend towards multiplex cinemas controlled by a powerful duopoly combined with exhibition practices produced an increase in the number of screens and an increase in cinema seats. Youth audiences were being attracted back to the cinema, and by 1989 there were 94.5 million admissions.

The exhibitors' second golden age was the late 1980s with the advent of out-of-town multi-screen cinemas. After the Second World War more than 1.6 billion tickets were sold each year, but the number had collapsed by 96% to 54 million attendances by 1984. Many blamed television and video for killing off cinema. But then in 1985 Britain's first multiplex cinema opened in Milton Keynes. Copied from America, the concept was a multi-screen cinema on the edge of town showing all the latest releases instead of just a few. By the end of that year there were 10 screens in multiplexes and by 2000 there were 1,875 out of a total of 2,954 cinema screens; the cost of the changeover was £500 million. But in terms of the number of screens, this was still less than half the number in the 1950s.

The multiplex revolution attracted Hollywood, and Rank and Cannon were joined by powerful interests who came to dominate the multiplex very quickly. They included United Cinemas International (UCI), owned by Paramount Communications, MCA, National Amusements (Showcase) and Warner Brothers. By the late 1980s Cannon had overextended itself, and its cinemas were absorbed by MGM Pathé, making them the largest operator in the UK; they owned 406 screens, 26% of all the screens in the UK (*BFI Handbook* 1992).

The success of video, the deregulation of European broadcasting, the introduction of new distribution systems like satellite and cable television, and new markets in Eastern Europe and the Far East were changing the structure of the industry and creating a massive new demand for films. So the 1980s were to see an explosion in film production, and in America new independent production companies raised substantial capital in the form of equity and junk bonds as well as lines of credit from banks, including First National Bank of Boston, Wells Fargo, Bank of America, and Credit Lyonnais. The pay-cable operators like HBO and Showtime and independent video labels like Vestron and Embassy Home Entertainment were competing for market share and offering not just advances but equity investment in films in exchange for distribution rights, which further boosted independent production. This growth in the media sector also attracted investors.

But every boom is followed by bust, and by the mid 1980s as more films were made and the American cable and video businesses consolidated, so prices paid by the TV networks fell. Theatrical advances remained steady but in real terms, allowing for inflation, they declined, while producers were facing increased costs as the demand for screenwriters, directors, actors and technicians spiralled. The return of the star system, and escalating fees, meant that production costs increased by some 30% in just a few years. For UK producers, fluctuating currency markets and a weak pound added to the risk. In November 1980 the pound stood at $2.40, reaching a low of $1.03 in

April 1985. Given a film project typically takes 18—36 months, such a fluctuation was a real problem.

GOLDCREST

Goldcrest began life in the late 1970s as a small film development fund founded by Jake Eberts and backed by the media group Pearson Longman. The success of David Puttnam's *Chariots of Fire* in 1981, based on Goldcrest's development funds, and Puttnam's growing reputation as one of the leading film producers in the world, led to bigger plans, and it became for just a few years the flagship for the British film industry.

Although Goldcrest's founding fortunes were widely held to be based on *Chariots of Fire*, which won four Oscars, including Best Picture, Goldcrest's role had been confined to developing the film. It had not been involved in making or marketing the film, which had been co-financed by Twentieth Century—Fox Studios and Allied Stars, a company controlled by Dodi Fayed, heir to the Harrods Emporium and later tragically killed with Princess Diana in Paris in 1997.

In *My Indecision Is Final*, Jake Eberts admitted there was no researched and carefully conceived business plan. It was a company built on vision, energy and opportunism, and for a few short golden years they did brilliantly. Its strategy was to follow creative talent, not themes; produce films for both the mass and specialised markets; retain foreign rights to maximise revenue; control production of the film to ensure quality; retain distribution flexibility; manage financial risk; and keep within its financial and operational capacity. Sophisticated tax-based funding was used, beginning with capital allowances and sale and leaseback deals and borrowing against pre-sales, and blue-chip City institutions invested in the company.

Market conditions helped. The new Channel 4 had production funds and needed to buy product from independent film-makers, US cable TV companies were competing for films, and weak sterling made UK films very cheap to buy, especially for US distributors.

The prospectus for Goldcrest's new film development fund, Goldcrest Films International (GFI), was issued in February 1980 and by July the limited partnership had raised £8.2 million. Pearson

Longman invested £3.6 million, holding 44% of the stock, and Electra invested £1.3 million. Their existing shareholdings in Goldcrest Films were rolled into GFI. The new shareholders included the National Coal Board Pension Fund, the Post Office Staff Superannuation Fund, Noble Grossart Investments Ltd, Thomas Tilling plc, and investment trusts managed by Murray Johnstone Ltd and J. Henry Schroder Wagg & Co. Critically, IFI owned 7.5% of GFI, which was intended to match the 9% IFI owned, via the $1 million investment through Firecrest, by Goldcrest. These cross shareholdings were later to make life very complicated for both parties.

The funding of GFI was a major step for Goldcrest, moving it from development investment into production investment and significantly increasing the scale of its operations. From being a bit-part player in the independent film industry, Goldcrest was on the threshold of success.

But only one of the directors at the first board meeting of GFI had any film-making experience. David Puttnam was seated with bankers, financiers and shareholders' representatives. This was no accident, because GFI was never intended to be a film production company, but a specialist venture capital fund focusing on the independent film sector, spreading the fund across a wide portfolio of film projects, and limiting the size of each investment. Innovative financing techniques were used with an emphasis on tax-leasing deals and aggressive rights management. The board were there to make financial and investment decisions, not to make creative or commercial assessments of different film projects. That job was left to Jake Eberts and Jo Childs, the respective heads of GFI and IFI.

Its biggest commercial success was *Ghandi* (directed by Sir Richard Attenborough and starring a then little-known actor, Ben Kingsley), which opened on 30 November 1982. For an investment of £5 million, Goldcrest's share of the box office was £11.5 million. The US television rights: network, pay-cable and syndication were sold for $20 million, the largest sum for a single picture deal at the time. The film won eight Oscars and the British press feted Goldcrest as *the* British film industry, EMI and Rank trailing in their wake. By 1990 the film had grossed $80 million, of which $32 million was available to Goldcrest, its co-financiers (Pearson and the Indian government), and profit participants including the director.

From that moment, top film-makers from around the world were pitching film projects to Goldcrest. But as the company grew, Jake Eberts and Goldcrest were growing apart as the company turned into a large business. In the summer of 1983 N.M. Rothschild and Sons was appointed to coordinate the restructuring of the complex partnership interests into a new company, Goldcrest Film and Television (Holdings) Ltd, and sponsor a £12 million fund-raising. The new company was formally opened for business on 4 May 1984, with a blue-chip investor base including Pearson (41%), the National Coal Pension Fund (10%), Electra Investment Trust (5.1%), and smaller investors such as Scottish Investment Trust, London and Manchester Assurance, Coral Leisure Group, Murray Investment Trust, and the Post Office Superannuation Scheme Venture Capital Fund. On the back of the equity fund-raising, Goldcrest secured a credit facility of £10 million from Midland Bank.

Even with substantial funding in place, Goldcrest still relied on partners, either co-financiers who shared the equity or distributors who put up advances prior to production. A key relationship was with Warner Brothers, the Hollywood studio to whom David Puttnam was also close. Warner was attracted not just by Goldcrest's track record and the pool of creative talent in the UK, but also by the favourable exchange rate, tax breaks and the long-established levy system that subsidised UK film productions.

The fund-raising was completed when the production programme was stalling. Goldcrest needed new product to distribute, and it set about creating a production programme, which in the words of Terry Ilott was 'certainly the most trumpeted, and arguably the most catastrophic, film investment programme ever undertaken by a British company' (Eberts and Ilott 1992, p. 315).

By 1985 Jake Eberts had left the company to form Allied Film-makers, which some in the industry thought was going to be another Goldcrest. But Eberts wanted to return to the original business of Goldcrest, as a packager and developer of films. He did not want to be involved in production finance or television. So he set about raising a $5 million development fund, and with Goldcrest's agreement, Electra became an investor and Warner would provide advances and underwrite Allied's overheads for three years. But as Goldcrest's fortunes declined, he was asked to return as chief executive within a year.

With a small production programme and receipts from its existing films coming in, the trading results to the end of 1984 reported Goldcrest's first profit — £1.6 million on a turnover of £14 million and average capital employed of £23 million. But these results were misleading, as the profit related to interest receivable on the equity funds raised and a technical adjustment in taxation. Although the company had large cash reserves and ambitious plans for a production programme, it had high overheads, a television production programme that was losing money, and a £1 million investment in a loss-making cable venture. The company needed to produce more hits.

GFI's investment risk was designed to be reduced by pre-sales and third-party participation. So GFI was applying investment criteria to film-making. If it had followed its own policy, it may have survived longer than it did.

Puttnam's influence on Goldcrest was profound from the beginning in 1980 to when he resigned in 1986 to join Columbia Pictures in Hollywood as chairman and chief executive; by this time Goldcrest was in serious financial difficulties.

Films like *Revolution*, with cost overruns and Goldcrest's biggest single film investment, cost in sterling terms as much as the combined costs of *Another Country, Gandhi, The Dresser, Local Hero* and *Cal*, and more than the company's entire turnover in 1984. But within weeks of shooting in March 1985, the film was already £1.2 million over its £16 million budget and it would end up costing £19 million. With no completion insurance in place, Goldcrest was at serious financial risk. It was then that the company moved from its functional office in Kensington to palatial offices in Wardour Street at a greatly increased rent, and with poor television revenues, increased administration costs and losses from its cable investment, Goldcrest was in serious financial difficulties.

The company needed to raise more funding, and a convertible loan stock was considered by existing shareholders. Talks were held with its bankers, Midland Bank, but the bank's terms were too onerous. James Lee, the chief executive and former director at Pearson, resigned and in August 1985 Jake Eberts was asked to resume a key role in the business. Goldcrest's financial position was deteriorating rapidly, and Eberts' time was frustratingly spent on vain attempts to refinance the company. The company's hopes hung on three films: *Revolution, Absolute Beginners* and *The Mission.*

As the company's difficulties became public, all kinds of approaches were made to Goldcrest with offers of money. But most proved to be time-consuming and abortive negotiations. Serious approaches were made, one in October 1985 from the Australian tax-shelter fund UAA, who had experience of the film industry. In return for a controlling interest of more than 75%, they offered to inject new funds into the company at the equivalent of 25 pence a share, which valued the existing shareholders' stake at £7 million. In addition they undertook to give the existing shareholders all the earnings from the three films still in production. But the board rejected the proposal, and the shareholders were not to receive an offer anywhere as good again.

Eberts set himself a deadline of 1 February 1986 to raise a target of $20–25 million of new equity, talking to institutional investors, Coca-Cola, and major European and US media groups. At that time, video companies would provide big advances to secure the US video rights to good films, and sometimes their advances were bigger than those for the US theatrical rights. By December 1985 it was clear that they could not raise funding from either the US or UK investment communities, and so the search was on to merge with another media company.

Potential merger partners like ITC (Robert Holmes à Court's film and television company), Virgin, Carlton Communications, advertising agency Saatchi & Saatchi and leisure and media group First Leisure were all discussed, but none made an acceptable offer.

The board's hope of being rescued by *Revolution* crashed when the film opened on Christmas Day 1986 in New York to terrible reviews. Two weeks later, sneak previews were held in Los Angeles of *Absolute Beginners*, and it soon became clear that it was another flop resulting in a £3.2 million write-off for Goldcrest. The board was split as to either winding up the company or to continue trading, but it was agreed to await the outcome of *The Mission* and to give the company one more year to find a buyer. Interim draft results at the end of June 1986 showed a half-year loss of £6.2 million, and the net worth of the company had fallen to £2.8 million, the equivalent of just 8 pence a share.

The new fund-raising having failed, Eberts stepped down a second time as chief executive in November 1986, just as an unsolicited approach was made by a US property developer, Earle Mack, who offered to inject £6 million into Goldcrest for an 85% controlling interest, leaving the receipts from *The Mission* to be divided among the existing shareholders. With hindsight, the offer was generous, but as it required the issue of new shares and so was a capital reconstruction, it required a 75% majority of the existing shareholders to approve the deal.

During this period *The Mission* opened on 4 October in Paris and Madrid. The film was to do moderately well at the box office and win critical acclaim, but it still resulted in Goldcrest having to write off £3 million, which in Eberts' words were the *coup de grace* to the company, leaving it technically insolvent with a negative net worth of £450,000. Overnight Mack's offer looked a good one.

A heads of agreement was signed in January 1987, and as news of the deal became known, counter-bids from Hemdale and Brent Walker were received by the board and expressions of interest were made by other companies including Virgin. Brent Walker via a company called Masterman made a formal offer in February, which was followed a week later by an offer from Hemdale, based in Los Angeles.

While Mack's offer was new money into Goldcrest, both Masterman and Hemdale were offering to buy out existing shareholders, and Masterman was offering more than Hemdale. For Mack's offer to be agreed, it required a majority of 75% of the shareholders to agree the deal. The vote was set for 3 July 1987.

Amazingly, despite both the management and staff plus key shareholders including Pearson and Electra wanting to accept Mack's offer, because it guaranteed Goldcrest's independence, the required vote fell short of the 75% majority of shareholders by a hair-splitting 0.6%. A minority of investors had vetoed the deal and left the way clear for Masterman and Hemdale. The only other alternative was liquidation.

The board was left with no choice but to invite offers from anyone, and set a date of 14 August for bids. By the end even Hemdale dropped out, which gave Masterman the company. On 20 August the board met and recommended the Masterman bid to the shareholders, and on 15 October the deal was formally approved at an extra-ordinary general meeting.

So Goldcrest lost its independence and was sold to Masterman, part of the Brent Walker leisure empire that was to collapse in the early 1990s. Masterman paid £4.9 million in cash, shares and warrants and assumed contractual commitments worth £3.3. million to support Goldcrest's existing film investments. For a total cost of £8.2 million Masterman received an existing cash inflow of £10.6 million, being its share of revenues from its films; the copyright to a valuable film library; accumulated tax losses of £33 million that could be set against their own tax liabilities; and Goldrest's brand name and reputation, exemplified by having been associated with films which received 40 Academy Award nominations and actually won 19 Oscars over a six-year period.

It was a very good deal by Masterman because the inherent value of Goldcrest's film library cost them nothing. In a period when the demand for screen entertainment was increasing, film libraries were becoming very valuable. Goldcrest's portfolio included 24 feature films, 12 television films, 7 television dramas and 8 documentary series. From the perspective of a majority of Goldcrest's shareholders, the company was sold to the wrong bidder.

So why did Goldcrest fail when it had produced a string of hits and had blue-chip investors? Diversifying into the less profitable production of miniseries for television (like *The Far Pavilions* which lost £2 million), bad investment decisions and uncontrolled overheads crippled the company. Also, its high-profile success attracted rivals and imitators and by 1984, Handmade Films, Virgin, a rejuvenated EMI and the London office of the US film and television company Embassy Pictures were all competing for British talent. The US was also seeing an explosion of new independent production companies who were competing for talent, ideas and finance, all aimed at the same audiences. Jake Eberts concluded that while all these were causes for Goldcrest's collapse, the fundamental reason why the company failed was because 'too much risk was spread across too few productions'.

Between 1980 and 1987 Goldcrest had invested around £90 million in British film and television productions and produced quality films with international appeal, which launched the careers of new talent. But its collapse seriously undermined the relationship between the British film industry and City investors, making it very difficult for independent film and television producers to raise finance until the mid 1990s, and then only because of National Lottery funding and generous tax concessions.

TELEVISION

After the box-office failures of *Raise the Titanic* and *On Golden Pond*, ITC was in the 1980s sold to the Australian tycoon Robert Holmes à Court. When he died shortly afterwards, Alan Bond acquired the company, and when his empire crumbled in the late 1980s amid allegations of fraud, ITC was bought by the management of its New York subsidiary. The management team then sold it to Polygram in Los Angeles, who in turn sold it to Carlton Communications, returning it to UK ownership. The mix of international owners of ITC illustrated the value and demand for quality media assets.

In 1981 Channel 4 was launched as Britain's fourth terrestrial television network. With no production facilities of its own, it aimed to broadcast films of independent producers. So for the first time in the UK, films could be produced directly for television. The channel's first chief executive was Jeremy Isaacs, and his discussions with David Puttnam resulted in a series of low-budget films financed by Channel 4 and from the sale of foreign rights. At last new directors and screenwriters were being given a chance and Puttnam set up his own television company, Enigma Television. But with limited finance and no sales facilities, Puttnam needed a partner and he turned to Goldcrest to set up a television production fund. Enigma secured a favourable deal with Goldcrest, which contributed to Enigma's overheads, paid him producer's fees and undertook to assist in financing his productions. By 1984 Puttnam accounted for 44% of Goldcrest's entire film and television investments.

Channel 4 Films was part of Channel 4's commitment to creating innovative programming. It helped to keep the British film industry alive for much of the1980s and 1990s. Since 1982 it has funded feature films on a larger scale than the BBC.

The explosion in terrestrial, cable and satellite television created new markets for films. Television rights became very valuable, and the values of film libraries holding classic films increased in the 1980s as large media groups wanted to buy content, especially films with a long shelf life which can be broadcast time and again.

CITY FUNDING

Goldcrest's high-profile failure and rescue was not the only reason for City financiers to withdraw in the late 1980s. The Scottish investment community also experienced reversals, and Murray Johnstone Ltd lost money on a disastrous film called *Gunbus*, whose failure contributed to Scottish investment funds withdrawing from film finance. These events served to undermine investor confidence in the industry, and other companies like Thorn-EMI, Virgin and Handmade began scaling back their activities.

Margaret Thatcher's dislike of government subsidies resulted in her government changing film's tax status and phasing out capital allowances by 1986. The Eady Levy was abolished by The Films Act 1985, and a 'withholding tax' was introduced for foreign stars working in the UK. Without subsidies and tax incentives, the investment climate was unattractive to city financiers.

The role of the Eady Fund was partially replaced by British Screen Finance, a private organisation supported by limited government grants, and in the late 1980s and early 1990s it supported new talent, promoting links with Europe and helping to finance film projects.

In 1985 some 54 films were produced in the UK, and in 1989 just 30. Even worse, the average budget was also falling. So by the late 1980s the British film industry was experiencing a slump, and it was not until the mid 1990s that City money would return to independent film and television production. For an independent producer in the late 1980s, the only source of funding seemed to be from America.

FILM FINANCE

Foreign investment was attracted by the tax break of 100% capital allowances, combined with a strong dollar, and the increased global demand for good movies. Between 1979 and 1986, when Chancellor Nigel Lawson phased them out, capital allowances were a major incentive for financiers. Films were treated like investing in plant and machinery. A company could write off against tax their entire investment in a film in the first year, and set off the allowance against its profits from other films. So providing a company produced successful films, it could keep investing tax-free into more films.

But the abolition of capital allowances and the Eady Levy and the decline of the dollar hit the British film industry hard. Goldcrest was facing serious financial problems and only escaped liquidation in 1987 by selling out to Brent Walker. Handmade Films was forced to scale down and was sold to Canadian interests. Virgin quit film production in 1986 and Palace stumbled on until it went into liquidation in 1992. Even Thorn-EMI Screen Entertainment was taken over by Cannon and ceased to be a production house of importance as Cannon focused on cinemas rather than films.

The NFFC ceased in 1985. In its 35-year life it had assisted over 750 films and become an important resource for many independent producers. The controversial Eady Levy was also abolished and many felt that it was the Americans producing in Britain who had taken the lion's share.

British Screen replaced the NFFC in 1986 as a private company with four shareholders: Channel 4, Granada Television, United Artists Screen Entertainment, and Rank. Its mandate was to develop treatments, draft scripts and then package a film to meet commercial objectives.

It seemed that American companies were happy to make big-budget films in the UK rather than finance British companies. But by the end of the decade, the industry was facing another slump and the period from 1988 to 1991 was particularly bad. From £142 million in 1984, American investment in British production more than halved to £67.8 million by 1993 (*BFI Handbook* 1994).

The 1980s saw new and innovative financing techniques. Pre-selling of distribution rights for cinema, cable and pay television, and video became a major source of production finance throughout the film world.

In August 1979 a statement of practice from the Inland Revenue (SP9/79) stated that films could be depreciated at the rate of 100% in the first year. Initially no distinction was made between British and non-British films, so if the production company was based in the UK, even foreign films benefited from the tax concession. To prevent what were unintended tax concessions for foreign companies, the concession was limited by section 72 of the Finance Act 1982, which stated that first-year allowances would no longer be available to overseas films with little or no British content, which in practical terms meant that the film did not qualify for Eady money.

These generous tax concessions to the film industry were originally only intended to last for two tax years to 31 March 1984. After much lobbying, the concession was extended for a further three years to 31 March 1987, and the government hinted that providing the concession was not abused, the intention would be for the film industry to continue to enjoy first-year capital allowances.

For tax and depreciation purposes, films were treated in just the same way as plant and machinery. Companies with taxable profits could write off their entire investment in a film in the year of its production. So providing a producer kept producing successful films, the profits of one picture could be relieved against the capital allowances for the next picture, resulting in tax being continually deferred.

This tax concession was fine for large companies who could set off 100% of the production cost against their other profits. But how could an independent producer use capital allowances when they had no other profits? This is where creative tax accountants and bankers applied tax structures from the sale and leaseback of aircraft and office blocks to the world of film. In simple terms, the film producer sold the film to a financier or company with taxable profits, and then leased the film back for an agreed number of years (up to a maximum of 15), and made regular monthly payments which covered the interest cost on the money and a repayment of capital. The tax advantage to the buyer was that it could set off the cost of buying the asset by claiming capital allowances and using that relief against its taxable profits. In addition to an immediate tax saving, the buyer also secured a stream of rental income. The advantage to the film producer was recovering all the production costs in the first year, and they could spread the payments over many years for the asset, and also set off those payments against tax. The UK Treasury was subsidising both the lessor and the lessee, who shared the monetary value of the tax concessions between them. A Barclays Bank subsidiary, Mercantile Industrial Finance, was active in providing lease finance, as well as other banks specialising in film finance.

Sean Connery's last *Bond* film, *Never Say Never Again*, with a budget of £33 million, involved lease finance. It was the biggest film syndication in the UK, even though it was American-financed. The financing was arranged via Albion Films, which was partly owned by Samuel Montagu, a City merchant bank. The syndication involved both UK and US institutions, including Midland Bank, European Banking Company, Manufacturers Hanover and First Chicago. Other financing structures could have been used like forming a film partnership or a joint venture, but the tax concessions meant it was more lucrative to engineer a sale and leaseback of the film.

The technical details behind such deals were very complex, and for a time the film industry offered lucrative work to the tax lawyers and accountants. Considerable attention was paid to tax indemnity and tax variation clauses in case tax rates suddenly changed to undermine the complex calculations on the capital and rental payments.

But by 1984 Nigel Lawson, the Chancellor of the Exchequer, began tightening the tax rules and the valuable tax benefits for both lessor and lessee were reduced. In his 1984 Budget, the Chancellor reduced first-year capital allowances from 100% to 75% for the tax year 1984–85, reducing again to 50% in the following year and nil for capital expenditure incurred on or after 1 April 1986. Other expenditure (not qualifying for first-year allowances) could be written down at the rate of 25% per annum. Together with increasing interest rates as the economy boiled over, this meant that leasing deals became far less attractive.

The impact of the withdrawal of these valuable tax concessions proved to be less than was feared, because they were both time-consuming and complex to use, as Goldcrest found when trying to raise lease finance for *Ghandi*. Al Clark, head of film production at Virgin Vision, a part of Richard Branson's Virgin empire, which in the early 1980s was one of the fastest-growing producers in the UK, was quoted as saying, 'The loss of allowances will restrict a number of things we can do and may well end up being a curb on what we can produce. Even so, capital allowances are not everything, they are just an extra incentive' (*Sight & Sound*, Summer 1984).

David Puttnam's Enigma Films, which relied on the NFFC and then Goldcrest for much of its funding, was against capital allowances because in effect they were an artificial tax device. He preferred to see a range of financial mechanisms to encourage film production, such as using the Business Expansion Scheme (later to be replaced by the Enterprise Investment Scheme), and allowing film costs to be an allowable expense against the levy for television companies. Even Channel 4 was relaxed about the phasing out of capital allowances. Its view was that reliance on a tax shelter was unhealthy for creativity.

In the late 1980s the European Commission created MEDIA (Measures to Encourage the Development of the Audio-visual Industry), a programme designed to encourage collaboration between film and television across Europe, with an Ecu 250 million fund spread over five years. The first stage of the programme, MEDIA I, comprised 20 schemes to encourage producers in each member state. The number of schemes was to be cut back in the second stage of the programme, MEDIA II, during the 1990s.

OTHER PRODUCERS

British production revived between 1983 and 1985 with the success of Goldcrest, Handmade Films, Palace Pictures, Virgin and Working Title. The independents' success and burgeoning British talent once again attracted the US majors. A string of critical and box-office successes were produced, including *Chariots of Fire* (1981), *Gandhi* (1982), *Local Hero* (1983), *A Passage to India* (1985) and *A Room with a View* (1986).

Merchant Ivory Productions (MIP) was founded in 1961 by producer Ismail Merchant and director James Ivory. Their first feature film was from the novel of Ruth Prawer Jhabvala, *The Housebuilder*, a collaboration which was to prove long and successful, with Jhabvala scripting 19 MIP productions and winning two Oscars for her E.M. Forster adaptations, *A Room with a View* (1986) and later with *Howards End* (1992).

Like Goldcrest, which for a time became a film brand, Merchant Ivory has become a brand in its own right, crafting a series of inexpensive, lucrative period pieces attracting critical acclaim. They work with leading British actors including Anthony Hopkins, Vanessa Redgrave, Emma Thompson, Maggie Smith and Helena Bonham-Carter. Merchant has a reputation for producing films within tight budgets.

With offices in India, New York, London and Paris, Merchant traditionally negotiates with backers on a picture-by-picture basis. Despite signing a 'first-look' deal with Buena Vista in 1992, it places films with foreign sales companies like Largo Entertainment and Mayfair Entertainment, and other studios, including Warner Brothers and Sony Pictures Entertainment.

FILM STUDIOS

Against a brief renaissance in the British film industry in the wake of Goldcrest's success, the film studios were suffering, particularly by the late 1980s. Less than 50 films were made at Pinewood in this decade, although many were big-budget movies, including *Superman 3*, the *James Bond* films *Octopussy*, *A View to a Kill* and *The Living Daylights*, *Batman*, David Puttnam's production of *Memphis Belle*, and Ridley Scott's expensive flop *Legend*.

With the demise of the film industry, the film studios were turning their attention to television and commercials. In 1987 Pinewood, owned by Rank, followed its competitors and converted from being a fully serviced studio to a 'four-waller', an industry term meaning that just the space was rented, and all the support and technical staff were hired on a freelance basis.

CHAPTER 11

The 1990s

The early 1990s repeated the lean years of the 1980s, but a combination of box-office hits, tax concessions by the new Labour government in 1997 and subsidies from the National Lottery transformed the industry, so by the end of the century the British film industry is booming and more importantly, being restructured. Film finance benefited from major reforms, with important tax concessions and a new source of funding via the National Lottery stimulating the industry. Cash-rich insurance companies also entered the market with sophisticated film insurance policies.

The UK film industry prospered in the 1990s with a string of successful films, including *Four Weddings and a Funeral, The Madness of King George, Bean, The Crying Game, Trainspotting, The Full Monty, The English Patient*, and *Lock, Stock and Two Smoking Barrels*. In box-office terms, the most successful film was *Notting Hill*, which in 1999 grossed $350 million. Its success has started another trend of UK film-makers raising the international appeal of their films by hiring big Hollywood stars. In 1998 UK films earned the biggest revenues of all the European films released across Europe.

The dominance of the American market influenced British film-makers to launch their own productions in America. In 1994 the distributors of Working Title's *Four Weddings and a Funeral* launched the film in America, which resulted in the ironic situation of one of the most successful box-office hits in British cinema history being advertised in its home market as 'America's No. 1 Smash Hit Comedy'.

The advent of new media – digital, cable, satellite television – was increasing the demand for content. The value of film libraries continued to increase as films are screened in new distribution channels and digitalised and edited. Simon Parry, chief executive of British Screen Finance, the privatised company which channels loans and grants to films, was quoted by the *Financial Times* as saying in May 1997, 'I have worked in the business for 25 years, and I have never known a better time for stories to be written, and films to be made.'

Box-office hits and growth in the British film industry have attracted more sophisticated tax-based financing techniques, and tempted by arrangement fees and high interest rates, new specialist funding groups have entered the film financing market, companies such as Newmarket Group, LLC and MM Media Partners, in addition to some banks who have not traditionally been active in the sector.

THE INDUSTRY

With rising cinema attendances, both the exhibition and distribution channels came to be dominated by American interests (Table 11.1).

Table 11.1. *Number of cinema screens in the UK 1989–99.*

	1989	1991	1993	1995	1997	1999
Multiplex screens	285	516	625	732	1,103	1,624
Other screens	1,139	1,126	1,223	1,271	1,280	1,201
Total	1,424	1,642	1,848	2,003	2,383	2,825

Source: Cinema Advertising Association

The trend for more multiplexes continued with greater concentration and intensification of American interests. In the 1990s the number of cinema screens in the UK almost doubled. By 1993 the majority of multiplexes were owned by MGM, Odeon, UCI, Warner Brothers and Showcase. The Hollywood majors now had a greater control over distribution in the UK than they were permitted by law in the US. The British Film Institute (BFI) expressed concern, and the Monopolies and Mergers Commission (MMC) reported that 'all the leading exhibitors except Odeon have some ownership link, direct or indirect, with a Hollywood studio' (MMC 1995). The report concluded, just like previous investigations into monopoly in the British film industry, that although it was a matter for concern, the extent of the monopoly did not raise worries for the public interest.

The growth in the number of screens in the UK in the latter part of the 1990s was unparalleled in the post-war era. But the number of screens can be misleading, as shown by Table 11.2.

Table 11.2. *Number of cinema screens per million population.*

	1996	1999*
France	112.0	125.0
Italy	77.0	82.0
Republic of Ireland	61.0	63.0
Germany	49.0	53.0
UK	37.6	47.4

* These figures are estimates made by Key Note

Source: Cinema Advertising Association and Key Note

So with still fewer screens per million people in the UK than other major European countries, multiplex sites made up the majority of screens in the UK and by 1998 accounted for 67% of cinema admissions (**www.dodona.co.uk**). The 1990s saw a boom with cinema admissions rising to their highest level since 1970. According to *Screen Digest*, in 1988 admissions were 84 million, by 1996 they were 125.1 million, and by 1999 they were 140.3 million, with a UK box office taking £643 million. In terms of the number of screens compared to the population, the UK has 47 screens per million of population, which when compared to some other European countries, is low.

It is the video market that has become an important channel for feature films. Video retail and rental sales figures from the British Video Association (BVA) demonstrate the value of video rights to a producer (Table 11.3).

Table 11.3. *UK video retail and rental sales 1990–99.*

	Retail units (million)	Retail value (£m)	Rental transactions (million)	Rental value (£m)
1990	40	374	277	418
1991	45	440	253	407
1992	48	506	222	389
1993	60	643	184	350
1994	66	698	167	339
1995	73	789	167	351
1996	79	803	175	382
1997	87	858	161	369
1998	100	940	186	437
1999	96	882	174	408

Source: British Video Association

The BVA estimates that the total video rental market, including rentals from all retail shops, is around 8% higher than the stated figures. The figures for 1999 show a fall in both the value and volume of sales in the retail and rental markets as DVD (digital versatile disc) becomes more popular.

The importance of the video market is such that in 1998, three UK films – *Mistress of the Craft*, *Sunset Heights* and *Underground* – went straight to video, without first being released to either cinemas or television channels. This direct-to-video distribution channel is likely to increase in the future.

As Sarah Street comments, 'It is ironic that the duopoly of Rank and EMI, whose existence had been tolerated by the government as a bolster against American domination, was finally broken by American companies – UCI, MGM Cinemas, Warner Theatres, and National Amusements' (Street 1997). By 1992 they controlled 77% of the UK market (*BFI Handbook* 1994).

The profile of audiences was also changing, with cinema-goers comprising a broader range of people and age groups, who are visiting cinemas more frequently. US-financed films and US-backed distributors and cinema owners still predominate, although the average budget of UK films is increasing.

In terms of economic value to the UK, the Office for National Statistics (ONS) estimates that the economic value added by film and video production and distribution, combined with cinema exhibition, was £1.96 billion, or 0.26% of total gross value added of the UK (Selwood 2001, p. 300).

According to Key Note estimates, consumer expenditure on films through the purchase of cinema tickets and the sale and rental of videos totalled £2.18 billion in 1999, of which cinema ticket sales accounted for just 24.5%. If subscriptions to BSkyB's movie channels are included, then the total consumer expenditure on feature films is estimated at nearer £3.5 billion. BFI has calculated that in 1996 consumers spent £1.3 billion on subscriptions to BSkyB's movie channels, and by 1999 this is estimated to have increased to £1.4 billion. These figures show an important trend, that people are increasingly watching films in their homes rather than the cinema. This explains why many television companies are now investing in feature film production.

The industry is also an important employer. ONS estimates that by 1996 there were 34,500 people employed in the film and video industries in the UK, with actors, producers and directors accounting for 21% of the total.

In *The Film and Television Industry 2000*, a report by Schober Direct Marketing, there were 85 film production companies in the UK, of which only 20 had profits of £1 million or more.

FILM PRODUCTION

In the absence of any official statistics on film production and investment in the UK, a record of film-making comes from data compiled by the trade papers *Screen Digest*, *Screen International* and *Screen Finance*, and the British Film Commission (Table 11.4).

The 1990s showed the changing nature of films being produced in the UK. In earlier decades, films were either small UK productions or big-budget US productions. Now mid-range films are being produced for the international market by international financiers and sales agents. Film financing can be classified into four categories:

wholly-financed UK productions, majority UK productions, minority UK productions, and overseas productions.

Table 11.4. *Number of UK films produced and their cost at current and constant 1999 prices.*

	Number of films	Current prices (£m)	Production cost in 1999 (£m)
1990	60	217.4	280.2
1991	59	243.2	294.1
1992	47	184.9	215.1
1993	67	224.1	260.7
1994	84	455.2	518.3
1995	78	402.4	454.7
1996	128	741.4	809.3
1997	116	562.8	509.9
1998	88	509.3	525.0
1999	92	506.5	506.5

Source: *BFI Film and Television Handbook 2000*, based on figures from Screen Finance/BFI and Key Note. Figures for 1999 are from *Screen Digest*

The number of big-budget movies being shot in the UK is falling because of increasing competition from other production locations such as Germany, Australia and Canada. Australia has attracted two *Star Wars* prequels and *Mission Impossible II* away from the UK.

Feature films are being financed by a combination of investment from distributors, broadcasters, sales agents, banks, investors (institutional and private) and lease finance. Sales agents are the new financiers on the block, as traditionally they only became involved when the film was completed.

Companies like Winchester, Renaissance and Film Four are building catalogues of film rights on the back of output and co-financing deals. The days of setting up a new production company for each film produced are not fully gone. Rather than working solely for a production fee, producers now try to build a company which acquires stakes in film development and production projects that will produce revenues. But UK independent producers are still undercapitalised and have to sell all the rights to the film to raise the funding, fore-going potentially valuable future streams of income.

At the end of 1998, *Screen Digest* estimated that there were 221 active film production companies in the UK, and of those 166 companies who had found a location to film, 86% were based in and around London.

Supported by the private equity group Candover Investments, Ridley and Tony Scott acquired Shepperton Studios and The Mill, a special effects production facility which produced the special effects for Ridley Scott's blockbuster *Gladiator*. They later merged this with Pinewood Studios, acquired from Rank by a management buy-in consortium.

TELEVISION

The BBC and Channel 4 are increasingly influential in film finance. In 1999 BBC Films and Film Four backed a combined total of 19 films for around £70 million (*Screen Digest*, February 2000). BBC Films was created in the 1990s to invest in theatrical movies, and their investment has been increasing every year. Its most famous film is *Mrs Brown*, the story of Queen Victoria and her gillie, starring Judi Dench and Billy Connelly. Recent films backed by the BBC include *Kingdom Come and Love*, and *Home & Obey*, which was released via United International Pictures in April 2000.

Channel Four Television Corporation, via its film-making subsidiary Film Four Ltd, has been a major investor and producer of feature films for twenty years. Its catalogue includes *My Beautiful Launderette*, *The Crying Game*, *Four Weddings and a Funeral*, *Trainspotting*, *Fever Pitch*, *The Acid House* and *East Is East*. Channel Four Television is the largest buyer of independently made films, including documentaries, in the UK terrestrial network. In 1998 it showed nearly 2,500 hours of independent productions, the same as the total number of hours of independent productions shown by all the ITV franchises and BBC1 and BBC2.

Films financed by the BBC and Channel 4 usually receive a cinema and video release before being shown on terrestrial television. Channel 4 is a fully vertically integrated film business, starting with script development to producing films for its own distribution channel, which is pay-TV on Sky and cable television. ITV's influence has declined, although Granada has a film production subsidiary, Granada Films, and Carlton owns several post-production companies to service the film industry.

BSkyB, the satellite broadcaster, has started investing in films through Sky Pictures, which invests in films via output deals with production companies. It started by screening films on television before cinema release, and now plans to become a studio in its own right and build its own film catalogue. In late 1999 it made a commitment to invest £25 million.

In March 1997 Channel 5 was launched as Britain's fifth and last analogue terrestrial television network. The licence had been awarded by the Independent Television Commission in October 1995 to Channel 5 Broadcasting, a consortium including media groups MAI, Pearson, CLT and the investment bank E.M. Warburg Pincus.

Its launch provoked intense competition for film and television rights between the terrestrial networks in the UK. The new channel needed to buy content, and so agreed to buy hundreds of hours of programming from the BBC's archive. Channel 5, with an annual budget of £110 million, is in direct competition with the other networks for buying film rights, and prices for licensing film libraries have increased. In April 1997 Channel 5 beat ITV by paying £87 million for a package of 190 films from Warner Brothers International Television, including exclusive first-run rights to Warner's film library for 1997 and 1998. Titles include *Batman*, *Lethal Weapon* and *Dangerous Liaisons* (*Broadcast Weekly*, 11 April 1997). In December 1999 Channel 5 paid more than $20 million to Warner Brothers for a further package of movies, buying the exclusive terrestrial rights to premiere all its 1999 releases, which will start to air from 2002 (*Broadcast Weekly*, 3 December 1999).

Feature films have formed a central plank in the Channel 5 schedule, and are broadcast every evening at peak time. After disappointing viewing figures when Channel 5 was attracting less than 3% of the viewing audience, the channel scored its highest ever audience when it screened *Independence Day* with an estimated 4.98 million viewers, a 24% share of the total viewing audience. Jeff Ford, Channel 5's controller of acquisitions, announced 'In just two years

Channel 5 has become the leading terrestrial channel for films' (*Broadcast Weekly*, December 1999).

DISTRIBUTION

On average there are around 50 active distributors in the UK theatrical distribution sector (Hancock 2000). The five major American studios still account for over 80% of exhibition revenues, with the balance shared between local distributors, such as Pathé, Entertainment, Film Four, and newcomers like Icon and Redbus.

Distribution continued to be dominated by American companies like Buena Vista, Columbia, Fox, UIP and Warner Distributors. In 1993 independent distributors who handled British films included Entertainment, First Independent, Guild and Rank Film Distributors.

Controlling distribution and the cinemas was supported by huge marketing spends on US films. So independent film producers not only had to fight for screens, they could never afford to match the marketing budgets of Hollywood. But occasionally, clever advertising campaigns were successful, such as Palace's marketing of *Company of Wolves* in 1984, or low-budget films like *The Full Monty* and *Four Weddings and a Funeral*.

With limited access to distribution and low marketing budgets, independent producers needed help. In 1988 the European Commission's MEDIA 92 EFDO scheme was launched to provide interest-free loans to help with the predistribution costs of low-budget films. It was to make available £100 million, and British films that received soft loans included *Distant Voices*, *Still Lives*, *Drowning by Numbers* and *Orlando* (Street 1997).

In the early 1990s the British film industry was no more than a low-budget producer, with an average budget of £2 million in 1992 falling to a low of just £1.8 million in 1993. By 1996 the average spend per film was £1.6 million, and by 1998 this had increased to £2.5 million. European co-productions have not been successful either.

In the 1990s the main sources of funding for independent producers were British Screen, the European Co-Producers Fund, the BFI Production Board, Channel 4, ITV and the BBC. Television companies were to become an important source of funding. Between 1982 and 1993 Channel 4 invested a total of £98 million in 273 films. The BBC has been investing on a smaller scale in films since the 1970s. By the 1990s the BBC Films Unit had an annual budget of £5 million to co-finance five films intended for cinema release. It also buys television rights of independently produced films.

After Lew Grade's disastrous foray into big-budget movies, and with a highly competitive market increasingly dominated by the Hollywood majors, ITV companies were absent from providing film finance until mid 1996 when plans were announced for ITV invest-ment of £100 million in British Films (*Screen International*, July 1996). Cable and satellite TV and pay-TV channels like BSkyB created an enormous appetite for films on the small screen.

Demand for videos and retail chains like Blockbuster have fed a consumer market hungry for movies. In 1991 the sales from UK retail and sell-through reached a peak of £1.18 billion (*BFI Handbook 1995*). But just like film distribution, the main video distributors are American-dominated, by Warner Home Video, Columbia Tristar and CIC, and by 1993 the video rental top 20 comprised entirely American films. Again, in 1994 all the top films were American with the exception of *Four Weddings and a Funeral*.

In 1995 the Tory government announced that National Lottery funds would be used to finance film production. The film industry welcomed the news against a background of declining budgets and disappointing European co-productions. In the summer of 1996 a report prepared by the National Heritage Department's advisory committee on film finance, chaired by the investment banker Peter Middleton, made wide-ranging recommendations to stimulate private investment in the film industry.

BSkyB supports many films, but in the mid 1990s it restricted its advance to £350,000 for a British film. Independent producers were back into the trap of seeking finance for one-off projects, and then totally dependent on a distribution system controlled by major American companies with their own product. So by the 1990s, with the exception of Working Title's stable of successful films and the three franchised studios funded by the National Lottery, some com-mentators believed independent British cinema was still no more than a cottage industry.

Some British films with international and domestic appeal prospered like *Howard's End* (1992) and *Shallow Grave* (1993). So-called crossover films like *The Crying Game* (1992) started out as an art-house film and went on to mainstream cinema.

For independent producers, distribution continues to be a challenge and there are many UK-made films that never make it to the big screen. The BFI estimates that only 15.5% of UK films 'managed a full release' in 1997, defined as a film playing on 30 or more screens around the UK within one year of production. It also estimated that around 69% of UK films remain unreleased a year after production and that 43% of films produced in 1997 were still unreleased in 1999.

FILM FINANCE

In the 1990s film financing came from the following sources:

- Television companies comprising Channel 4, BBC Worldwide, and BSkyB
- UK-subsidised bodies such as the Arts Councils of England, Scotland, Wales and Northern Ireland
- The National Lottery
- The new Film Council formally launched in April 2000 and set up by the Department of Culture, Media and Sport
- Continental and media companies operating in the UK
- UK investors, both institutional and private
- US film companies such as Miramax and Warner Brothers

During the 1990s Polygram Filmed Entertainment (PFE) was the largest single investor in UK films. In 1997 alone it invested £61 million. In 1998 PFE's parent, European electronics company Philips, sold it to Seagram Inc. of Canada, and a year later it was sold on to Universal Studios. PFE has now been renamed Universal Pictures International (UPI) and is no longer a source of funding for UK films. Although PFE's major subsidiary, Working Title Films, remains part of UPI, the demise of PFE leaves a gap in the UK film industry.

In December 1999 Universal Studios announced that it would not distribute films through UPI but through a joint venture company with US-based Paramount Studios called United International Pictures, a decision greeted with dismay by UK film-makers.

PUBLIC FUNDING

The only significant public funding agency was the public/private partnership British Screen Finance. Its shareholders were United Artists Screen Entertainment, Channel 4, Rank and Granada, with the government providing grants of £2 million a year, and additional funds being raised from loan repayments.

British Screen proved to be a successful financier in terms of the sums repaid by producers after a film's release, averaging above 50% of the amount granted. In 1997–98 British Screen granted around £5–6 million to selected films, a relatively small sum compared to other European countries and particularly France, where public funding amounts to over one-fifth of overall investment in film production (Selwood 1999, p. 203).

The mid 1990s saw radical changes in public funding for the film industry, with National Lottery funding and three film franchises being granted. In 1996 John Major's Tory government proposed investing lottery funds into the film production sector, and asked for consortiums to be formed comprising film production, distribution and sales companies to bid for lottery funding on a franchise basis.

The fund was eventually set up by the culture secretary, Chris Smith, when Labour came to power in 1997. His rationale was that by enabling film-makers to qualify for bigger grants he was paving the way for greater long-term studio investment and profitability. According to one source, a spokesman for the Department of Culture, Media and Sport said, 'The idea of lottery funding for films is not about picking guaranteed winners. It's about trying to fill a gap in finance that has made life very difficult for British film-makers for a long time.' Just as well, as the three franchisees soon earned a record for producing flops.

This initiative of using lottery funding to create mini studios came at a time when the British film industry was doing well. Film production was at its highest level for twenty years with a string of successful films including *The Crying Game, The Madness of King George, Four Weddings and a Funeral*, and *Trainspotting.*

The film *Wilde* was released in October 1997, starring Stephen Fry as Oscar Wilde. At that time it was the most heavily subsidised British film ever released, with a loan of £1.5 million from the National Lottery (*Financial Times*, 11 October 1997). The practical impact of lottery funding was to increase the number of film projects in development and production; there was an increase in demand for film technicians and their pay rates went up.

In 1998 the government awarded three companies lottery-backed six-year franchises to encourage them to create three film studios and to make commercially viable films 'of benefit to the public'. They shared £90 million of lottery money; this represented 20% of the films' budgets, which totalled £450 million. The franchises can only use lottery funds to make British films, a term which was defined in the Films Act 1985. The three studios are DNA Film Ltd, The Film Consortium and Pathé Productions.

DNA Film Ltd

Based in London, DNA Film Ltd received £29 million. In 2001 it released *Beautiful Creatures* starring Rachel Weisz, a £4 million black comedy which bombed at the box office. Run by Duncan Kenworthy, who made *Notting Hill*, and Andrew Macdonald, who produced *Trainspotting*, they are free to produce films with strong commercial prospects for foreign studios, while reserving the least popular subjects for lottery funding. They plan to make a total of 16 films at a rate of approximately three a year, with a budget of up to £4 million per film. DNA has a worldwide distribution agreement with Universal Pictures International.

The Film Consortium

The Film Consortium (TFC) comprises four companies: Greenpoint Films, Parallax Pictures, Scala Productions and Skebra Films. It received £33.55 million and pledged itself to produce 39 films, making around four to five films a year on budgets from £1.5 million to £6 million. Three years later TFC had made just five films, all dismal flops, and still its franchise was renewed for another three years, although termination was threatened because of the company's poor record. In August 2000 TFC was sold to the quoted group Civilian Content plc (CC), a former meat processing company. CC paid £1 million for TFC, and CC will receive lottery funding of £20 million. It aims to move into direct distribution in the UK, handling its own films and the output of other independent UK film companies. Despite TFC performing 'below expectations', the franchise was renewed after a six-month review by independent advisers KPMG and solicitors Allen & Overy. The decision was announced by the Film Council, and justified by the change in ownership and additional management skills of Civilian Content plc.

Pathé Productions

Based in France, Pathé Productions was formed by six producers and their companies in association with Pathé Pictures. It received £33.12 million on the strength of the promises made by producers of movies such as *Ghandi*, *The Killing Fields* and *Dangerous Liaisons*. The companies are Imagine Films and Thin Man Films, Allied Filmmakers and Allied Films, NFH, Pandora Productions, Sarah Radclyffe Productions, Fragile Films, and MW Entertainment. Pathé has committed to making 35 films, and it already has one critical and commercial success, *An Ideal Husband*.

How the system works

This system was initially administered by the four national Arts Councils for England, Wales, Scotland and Northern Ireland. In October 2000 a government quango serving as a unified film agency for England and Wales, the Film Council (chaired by Alan Parker and whose members include Joan Bakewell and the chief executive John Woodward), was established to control the lottery millions being spent by the three franchisees. Its first task was to review the franchises, which were effectively multimillion-pound lottery handouts.

The Film Council took over responsibility for lottery grants from the Arts Council in October 2000. It brings together all the public funding organisations and has its own budget for the next five years.

The industry has high expectations. Robert Murphy, editor of *British Cinema in the 1990s,* commented that since 1997 the government now recognises that film-making is an economic activity as well as a cultural one.

Central government funding worth £17 million a year in 1999 also flows to the British Film Institute, which is responsible for promoting awareness about the cinema. Public funds to assist the film industry also flow to British Screen Finance, a film production funding agency that controls the European Co-Production Fund, the National Film and Television School, and the British Film Council and its regional offshoots. European agencies like the European Audiovisual Observatory based in Strasbourg also benefit from public funding.

Until 1995 a pan-European co-production fund, Eurimages, provided production funding to UK producers. The government then withdrew and has concentrated on attracting producers from the US and other countries to use locations and the post-production facilities in the UK.

The UK also benefits from European funding for the film industry as a member of the European Commission's MEDIA programme. MEDIA I consisted of 20 programmes to promote the film industry. MEDIA II is a five-year programme designed to support the film, television and multimedia industries in becoming more competitive by promoting development, distribution and training . With a budget of around £205 million, the funding provides grants and interest-free loans to independent film production and distribution companies. One of its funding organisations, the European Media Development Agency, based in London, distributed over £12 million each year to European producers for development funding and scriptwriting support.

From 2001 the programme was replaced by Media Plus for the next five years, and this new programme will have more funding as the European Union recognises the importance of audio-visual creation and exploitation (Selwood 2001, p. 304). The result of these initiatives is that there has been a modest increase in the late 1990s of co-productions involving UK producers.

By 1999 the UK film industry produced 92 films at a cost of £506.5 million, one of the best years for the UK film industry (*Screen Digest,* June 2000). This accounted for 13% of films made in the European

Union in that year and 32% of total EU investment in film-making. Compared to other European countries, the UK makes fewer co-productions, with 28 co-productions in 1999 compared to 90 in France (half its output) and 30 in Germany (41% of its total output).

At last, the film industry is being seen by government as a way of promoting the country abroad. The British Council, the cultural arm of the Foreign Office, actively promotes British film overseas and publishes an annual review of British film production. The British Film Commission, founded in 1992, is an agency to assist film-makers shoot and produce films in the UK. It has seen inward investment in UK film-making increase from £59 million in 1992 to £251 million in 1998.

BUSINESS SPONSORSHIP

Unlike product placement in films, business sponsorship as a form of film finance is rare. Television series began in the early 1990s to be sponsored by companies − *Rumpole of the Bailey* was sponsored by a drinks company − and film festivals depend on corporate sponsorship. Two banks, Barclays and National Westminster Bank, are active funders of film and television projects, and Barclays contributes to campaigns promoting film. Film processing companies Kodak and Fujifilm sponsor films at the international level and this cascades down into local festivals and film literature.

PRODUCT PLACEMENT

It started with a back-lot deal with an opportunistic prop crew to place products in a film. By the end of 2000, product placement, where brand owners tie their products into a film, was generating $500 million a year. In *Goldeneye*, James Bond, played by Pierce Brosnan, was driving a BMW Z3 roadster rather than the traditional Aston Martin. *The World Is Not Enough* and *Austin Powers: The Spy Who Shagged Me* set new standards with endless plugs for a range of products from Heineken to Virgin.

Not all films pay for the privilege of displaying a known brand. *Cast Away* is set around a FedEx plane that crashes. FedEx did not pay a penny to have Tom Hanks portray one of its executives as a hero.

Even films with less salubrious contexts can attract product placement. In Sarah Polley's *Go!* the drug dealer's flat is dominated by a giant Bose sound system. From the product angle, providing the product itself is not used in the film to kill or harm, then from the brand-owner's perspective, the display of its product in the film is positive. It is generally considered bad publicity for a product to be used as an offensive weapon. Alcohol brands are a special case, because drinks companies do not need to be seen to follow a strict moral line, as alcoholism is a subject for all.

Today all major US studios and some smaller film production companies employ in-house marketing executives to seek out brands to place into a film. Generally, no fee is paid by the brand-owner; however, there's a mutual benefit for the tie-in between the product name and the film, as each promotes the other, and each gets exposure in new places. Some tie-ins will require brands to pay for television or billboard advertising that a small film could not afford by itself.

Tie-ins tend to be national rather than international, simply because there are so few truly global brands. So it is important for the brand-owner to find the right synergy between the brand and the film. It's called 'lateral marketing'.

Occasionally big money will be paid. James Bond fans were upset when Pierce Brosnan drove a BMW Z3 in *Goldeneye*, a 7 series saloon in *Tomorrow Never Dies* and a Z8 in *The World Is Not Enough*. The German motor manufacturer had paid the producers an estimated £80 million for the tie-in. Then in 2001, for the twentieth *Bond* film to reunite Aston Martin with James Bond, Ford Motor Co. has paid a rumoured £100 million to Metro-Goldwyn-Mayer and Eon Productions, the *Bond* distributors, to replace BMW. Ford considers the tie-in is vital to promote the launch of its new Aston Martin V12 Vanquish and to promote the Aston Martin brand.

In 2001 product placement formally entered the publishing world when British author Fay Weldon was commissioned by Bulgari, the Italian jewellers. For years authors had name-dropped and given their characters luxury cars and branded merchandise, and now a new literary genre is emerging combining fiction and blatant product placement. Ms Weldon, who has written two dozen novels, including *The Life and Loves of a She Devil*, was paid an undisclosed fee by the jewellers to write a novel that mentioned its name at least twelve times in a favourable light. The authoress went a stage further and based the theme of the novel around the product and called it *The Bulgari Connection*, a social comedy about women's relationship with jewellery. Bulgari published a limited edition of 750 copies of the book, which were given away in London and New York, and her publishers are launching the book in Britain and America later in the year. The reaction of other leading authors was positive.

PRIVATE FINANCE

The rejuvenation of the film industry in the 1990s has attracted private investment. Hermes Investment Managers has invested £65 million in Renaissance Films formed by Kenneth Branagh, which is involved in production, finance and sales. This investment is seen as a vote of confidence by a City institution in the UK film industry.

Independent producers are arranging finance from US and European companies. Aardman Animations, the producers of *Chicken Run*, are financed by Steven Spielberg's Dreamworks in Hollywood. In October 1999 Aardman signed a $250 million deal with Dreamworks to make five more animation films. Michael Rose, Aardman's head of film and TV, has said that this one deal secured the future of the company for the next decade.

Working Title Films has been described as the UK's most successful film production company, making a string of 1990s hits like *Four Weddings and a Funeral*, *Bean*, *Captain Corelli's Mandolin* and *Bridget Jones's Diary*. Since 1992 it has made 15 films costing a total of $193 million and grossed worldwide revenues of over $1 billion. Working Title was owned by Polygram Filmed Entertainment (now called Universal Pictures International) and was subsequently sold to Hollywood-based Universal Studios in 1999.

Eric Fellner and Tim Bevan, who run Working Title, have signed a five-year co-financing deal with UPI and the French media company

Canal Plus, whereby they can make five films a year with a budget of $25 million each. This is a generous contract and unique to the UK film industry.

Samuelson Productions Ltd, established in 1990, is another significant film company, having produced *Tom and Viv*, *The Commissioner* and *Wilde*. New distributors are emerging like Redbus Films (financed by Cliff Stanford, who made his fortune founding Demon Internet), Icon and Alliance.

THE TAX REGIME

Until 1997 most film production and acquisition costs were either written off over the income-producing life of a film, or set off pound for pound as the income arose. Alternatively, producers could claim relief at a flat rate of one-third of the cost per year when the film was completed.

Unlike the previous Conservative governments of Margaret Thatcher and John Major, a Labour government in 1997 proved to be a blessing for the British film industry, providing long-awaited tax incentives and following recommendations of the Middleton Committee in 1996. The Advisory Committee on Film Finance was set up to identify any obstacles to attracting private sector invest-ment into British Films, and the committee had recommended that a 100% write-off would have an immediate impact on investment in the film industry at a time when the industry was already doing well and so could exploit the tax concession. The committee also recommended that National Lottery money be used to create a Hollywood-style film structure to finance and distribute British films.

Sir Peter Middleton, with thirty years' experience at the Treasury and five years in investment banking, identified the basic problem of the British film industry. It was fragmented, with small independent companies who do not produce enough films to justify running their own distribution companies and are thereby excluded from the most profitable area of film-making. Investors are nervous of backing only one film as there is a high risk of it failing at the box office, or failing to find a distributor. His committee proposed a franchise arrangement to create a studio system where investors could back a portfolio of films like a venture capital fund.

Only eight weeks after taking office, Chancellor Gordon Brown's first Budget proved to be very generous, including tax breaks to increase annual investment in British films by £240 million, and Chris Smith, the Culture Secretary, changed Channel 4's finances so it could spend a further £16 million on making films in 1998 and 1999 (*Financial Times*, 11 October 1997).

A 100% tax write-off on film production and acquisition costs for British films with budgets up to £15 million was introduced, which enables the UK to compete head-on with the generous tax breaks for producers in Ireland. The tax write-off was available as soon as the film was completed; initially intended to run for three years, the scheme was subsequently extended. Tax relief is granted if the film earns a profit or, if a mini studio is the producer, the tax relief is allowable if the mini studio goes into profit.

Its impact was to reduce the cost of making films in the UK by allowing film-makers to recoup their investment earlier. To qualify for the tax concession, the film had to be certified as British by the Department of National Heritage under the Films Act 1985. This means that British studios have to be used for a high proportion of the film, and the production company must be registered, managed and controlled in the UK or another EU state.

The *Financial Times* reported research consultancy London Economics as predicting the new tax scheme could boost investment by more than 30% in the first year, create as many as 11,000 jobs and significantly increase exports. Wilf Stevenson, director of the British Film Institute, called it 'a real shot in the arm for the UK film industry. Until now, the UK was alone in Europe in not having some form of tax incentive aimed at levelling the field for film-makers' (*Financial Times*, 3 July 1997).

Sale and leaseback continues to offer tax savings and a valuable source of film finance for the independent producer. This applies to films with a budget of £1 million or more. At least 70% of the film's production costs must be spent in the UK and 70% of the labour costs must go to UK, EU or Commonwealth citizens. London Economics calculated the value of this tax break to UK film companies at around £30 million a year in 1997 and 1998.

Gordon Brown's March 2000 Budget announced the Corporate Venturing Scheme, a new initiative which also helps the film industry. This grants a tax relief rate of 20% to companies when investing in other groups whose royalties and licence fees are derived from intellectual property that they have created. As a film producer's only asset is its film and allied rights, UK film producers should become increasingly more attractive to corporate investors.

TAX PARTNERSHIPS

Complex tax rules allow the sale and leaseback of films and, traditionally, banks have bought the completed negative and associated rights to a film and leased them back to the producer.

Since 1997 film tax partnerships have been very successful with private investors, and more tax money has been available than the limited supply of qualifying British films. Investors can shelter unlimited amounts of income and capital gains in a virtually risk-free shelter of a sale and leaseback deal. Sponsors are now looking at qualifying television productions. But does the British film industry benefit? Film partnerships must buy a completed film, so producers who need to raise finance to get the film made do not benefit. Also, only about 10% of the money invested goes to the film industry and sometimes the quality of films being financed can be dubious. So while the schemes are very attractive to investors, the benefit to film producers is limited.

There are four film partnerships: Grosvenor; Matrix Film Britannia Partnership, UK Film Strategies and Voyager Film Partnership (Table 11.5). The Labour Budget of 1997 allowed newly created film partnerships to offset 100% of the investment in films against tax. But just like the old Business Expansion Scheme, when the tax rules are pushed to the limit of the wording of the statute and beyond the intention of Parliament, there is always the risk that the Inland Revenue will cry foul and spoil the party for everyone.

In these highly complex schemes, investors purchase interests in a partnership and invest 15–22% of the cost of the film with the balance being in the form of a loan from a financial institution. The loan is promptly placed on deposit with the same lending institution so there is in effect a risk-free 'back-to-back' loan from the bank's standpoint. The icing on the cake is that the scheme managers can take as much as 14% of the fund in administration charges. Which leaves just 6% of the fund to be invested in films. So financial and tax engineering creates tax relief for the investor, and the film industry gains far less than was intended.

Table 11.5. *Money invested in films by film partnerships.*

	Amount raised (£m)	
	1998—99	1999—2000
Voyager	44*	110
Grosvenor Park	51	130
UK Film Strategies	2	40
Matrix Film Britannia	0	44
Other privately marketed schemes	100	120
Allenbridge estimate of total market	197	444

* Plus £10 million returned that it could not find enough films to invest in

Source: *Tax Shelter Report*, no. 64, October 2000 and Allenbridge Group plc

The investor gains because his total investment can be written off against tax on the film's production, creating a tax loss, which the investor can set off against income tax or capital gains tax. The effect of the write-off is to give the investor an immediate cash injection equal to the difference between the cash put up by the investor and 40% of the total investment. But the investor has to wait for his tax relief until the film has been made.

From the independent film producer's perspective, film partnerships are definitely not a rich vein of finance because only a small part of the fund is invested directly into films, and anyway the partnerships want to buy existing product on a sale and leaseback basis. This is because the tax relief is not available until the film is completed and the Inland Revenue accepts it is a British-made film. So this generous tax break to investors does not even find its way to the producers of new films.

The Voyager Partnership is a recent example of what may be viewed as an aggressive tax avoidance scheme. Devised by investment advisers Pinder, Fry & Benjamin, they believe they are within the letter of the tax legislation. The scheme offers to pay 9% of the cost of the films chosen by the scheme. The producers must agree to pay back the 9%, plus a percentage of the film's profits, typically up to one-third. Films that have been refinanced in this way include John Boorman's *The General* and Lord Attenborough's *Grey Owl*.

Although these schemes are undoubtedly bringing new money into film, they are tax aggressive and there is a risk that the Inland Revenue may challenge them. Also, producers need money upfront rather than waiting for a sale and leaseback deal. Whenever the tax tail wags the commercial dog, there can be a curious twist. Because the film's income is first used to reduce the loan element of the film partnership, it creates a tax liability to be settled by the investor who has at that stage not received any of the money. So, perversely, if the film makes no money, the investor can be better off because there is no tax liability.

ENTERPRISE INVESTMENT SCHEME

Another tax concession which is being used increasingly by producers of low-budget films is the Enterprise Investment Scheme (EIS). Launched in 1994, EIS is a generous tax break to individuals who are tax-resident in the UK and to venture capital trusts. Investors who invest in ordinary shares in a qualifying trade which has assets of no more than £15 million, and film production is one, receive 20% income tax relief on their investment, and providing they hold the investment for a certain period, any gains from the investment are tax-free. If the investment is a dud, the loss can be set off against any other income or capital gains tax (CGT) liabilities the individual has in that tax year. The scheme is the government's way of promoting investment in high-risk ventures, and typically start-up or early-stage companies. Given that for every box-office hit there will be dozens of flops, EIS was tailor-made for the smaller producers in the film industry. Curiously, producers were slow to use the scheme, probably because it requires a prospectus to be drafted and issued to the public, a document which must comply with the onerous requirements of the Financial Services Act 1986.

There is no limit on EIS investment, but income tax relief for the investor is limited to £150,000 per year. CGT deferral can apply to any size of investment, as long as the EIS subscription is made within three years after, or one year before, the gain was realised.

Producers in both the cinema and the theatre have for a long time looked to private investors called angels for part of their finance. When more conventional sources of film finance failed, they realised the EIS could be used, and in addition to attractive tax breaks, investors have been offered the chance to feature as extras in the film or invited to premieres to meet the stars. From the producers' perspective, they can retain full creative control over the film because there is no one big shareholder.

By 1998 small independent producers were using the scheme, producers of films like *Paradise Grove*. Having been turned down for funding by British Screen and the National Lottery, the producers formed Paradise Grove plc and invited the general public to buy a minimum of £1,000 shares in the project, a comedy set in a Jewish old people's home. They raised £250,000, a tiny sum in film terms, but when combined with negotiating special fees with crew members and equipment suppliers and product placement deals, it was enough to begin production.

Other films to raise EIS funding include a production of Oscar Wilde's *An Ideal Husband* starring Sadie Frost; the historical drama *The Scarlet Tunic*; UK Films Group's *Mr Benn* starring John Hannah and marketed by Winchester Entertainment plc (*Financial Times*, 27 February 1997 and 7 October 1997). Winchester Entertainment, the quoted entertainment group, is using the EIS to raise £10 million for two independent films, and they expect them to be the first of many EIS-funded movies.

So while wealthy investors might be attracted to film partnerships for sheltering tax, film producers prefer the Enterprise Investment Scheme, which provides 100% of the investment funds. This is why the 1999 Budget offers some welcome news to the film industry because the EIS and CGT reinvestment relief have been brought together in a new unified scheme which encourages the channelling of new equity capital into high-risk trading companies like film production.

The new CGT relief to be introduced for serial entrepreneurs and investors in EIS companies both encourages and rewards reinvestment from one EIS company into another by offering more generous CGT taper relief for serial investors. Serial investors who defer a chargeable gain on the disposal of an EIS investment by reinvesting in new shares in another EIS company will benefit from taper relief on a cumulative basis. This new relief will apply where the shares in the first EIS company were issued after 5 April 1998 and disposed of after 5 April 1999.

GAP FINANCING

Another source of film financing is the trend in insurance-backed gap financing, where an insurer underwrites the bank loans that form part of the film's funding package, guaranteeing to compensate the producer for any shortfall between the sum insured and the money that the film makes. Reinsurers in turn insure 'direct' insurers. This form of financing has been around for years, and in the mid 1990s cash-rich insurance companies entered the market, insurers like American Insurance Group (AIG), Axa Reinsurance, and XL Capital, based in Bermuda (*Economist*, 31 March 2001).

As distributors are now less willing to buy a film unseen, a producer has to complete the film and valuable pre-sales income is limited. Film financiers buy an insurance policy, which provides them with a new kind of collateral to support a production loan advanced against sales estimates rather than advances payable under completed distribution agreements. Such insurance-backed gap financing may represent up to 30–40% of a film's total production budget (S.J. Berwin & Co. 2000). Underwriters require sales estimates from reputable and experienced distributors to form the basis of the risk against which any shortfall will be measured.

These policies cover the deficit if sales revenues fall short over a specified period of time, typically two years from delivery of the film to take into account revenue from the TV and video markets as well as the theatrical market. The policy pays out the financier for the shortfall between revenues actually received and the outstanding loan. The policies are expensive, with premiums typically between 8% and 14% of the insured amount. When claims have been made, insurers have sometimes disputed the claim on the grounds that relevant information was not disclosed, so some financiers have doubted the real benefit.

The problem was that many policies were written for one film at a time. When 9 out of 10 films lose money, the risk of failure and claims is high. In addition, insurers have often made the mistake of underwriting too high a percentage (sometimes as much as 50%) of the film's production budget. That was a disincentive for producers to watch what they spent.

The best known of the insurance deals in Hollywood was in 1995 when Mike Medavoy, a Hollywood veteran, was raising finance for Phoenix Pictures, his new production company. It wanted to finance five films, including *The People vs. Larry Flint* and *The Mirror Has Two Faces*. Chase Manhattan agreed to act as lead bank for a loan syndicate, and a group of insurers underwrote part of the financing package. But *Larry Flint* was a box-office failure, and *The Mirror* was doing well until its star, Barbara Streisand, demanded a huge marketing spend. The film then lost money, as did the other three films in the Phoenix package. This has resulted in litigation in London, with eight insurers, including HIH Casualty & General Insurance from Australia, and Lexington Insurance (a subsidiary of AIG), suing Chase and Heath Insurance Broking, the broker that placed the Phoenix policies.

Several insurers involved in similar deals with large losses have simply cut their losses. Axa Reinsurance is litigating with George Litto, a film producer, for revoking two insurance contracts for five films. Some insurers are still willing to underwrite film productions, but at a lower level. XL Capital spread the risk by insuring packages of at least eight films, cross-collateralising them, and then only up to 30% of the total budget. Another trend is for insurers to stall before they pay out on a claim, because the payback from a film can be many years. Some films only make money from foreign film sales and video rights.

The large claims that have been made under these policies have caused insurers' withdrawal from the market. Axa Reinsurance is reassessing its position after two years of mixed results in underwriting about 30 films. Kemper Reinsurance Co., American International Group, and Australia's HH Insurance are also holding back from writing new policies. Only General Star International

Indemnity, owned by US-based General Re Corporation, and Royal &
Sun Alliance are still underwriting policies. Between 1997 and 2000
it is estimated that film financiers in the US and UK have used
insurance-backed loans to provide $1 billion in financing films with
total budgets of at least $3 billion.

INDEPENDENT PRODUCERS

The 1990s saw a select few independent producers prosper. Merchant
Ivory Productions has led the way by becoming a respected brand in
its own right. Ismail Merchant explains: 'The strength of the company is that we've created a trade mark and people have always
associated our two names as one. Audiences are aware of what a
Merchant Ivory film is, so a sales agent knows that it will get *x*
amount of money. A certain value is created before the movie is
made' (*Screen International*, September 1996).

In the 1990s Merchant started backing films by other film-makers.
But while its period double *Howards End* (1992) and *The Remains of
the Day* (1993) became huge box-office and critical successes, box-
office success has since eluded them. *Jefferson in Paris*, *Feast of July*
(the second film under their Disney deal), *Surviving Picasso* and *La
Proprietaire* have all failed to live up to expectations.

Despite spasmodic box-office hits and the success of producers
like Working Title and Aardman Animations, life for the small
independent producer is still precarious. From 70 British films
released in 1999, just 10 took more than £2 million at the box office,
and 11 British films took less than £10,000 in ticket sales. The track
record in the first three years of National Lottery funding being
channelled into three franchises was very poor. But at least these
films have been screened. In 1997, out of 116 British films made in
that year, 33 still have no theatrical, television or video distribution
deals and have yet to be seen by the public.

In 2001 Working Title's £25 million production of *Bridget Jones's
Diary*, based on Helen Fielding's novel, took record opening receipts
for a British film and looks set to beat the box-office records of
previous blockbusters like *Four Weddings and a Funeral*, *Notting Hill*
and *The Full Monty*. Aardman Animations, producers of the Wallace

and Gromit films *A Close Shave* and *The Wrong Trousers*, signed a $250 million deal with Dreamworks to finance their next five films, a deal which safeguards the funding of the company for ten years. Intermedia produced *Sliding Doors*, and is producing Woody Allen's movie *Small Time Crooks*.

Cinema admissions hit a 27-year high in 2000, with more than 137.1 million tickets sold in the UK. This was up 3 million on 1999, due to more multiplex cinemas and Hollywood blockbusters like *Toy Story 2* and *Gladiator*. The last time this happened was in 1974, when there were 138 million admissions, attracted by big-budget productions like *Earthquake* and *The Towering Inferno*. Admissions are unlikely to match the post-war era again, when in some years more than 1 billion tickets were sold.

CHAPTER 12

Lessons from the Twentieth Century

This book could have been called 'Road to Dreams and Bankruptcy'. British cinema has staggered from one crisis to the next. If there has never been a golden age of British film-making, some years have seen flashes of brilliance, such as the 1930s, the early 1980s and the mid 1990s. At the end of the century, it has real strengths.

Although film and cinema were invented and industrialised in Europe, it was the American film moguls like Laemmle, Zukor and Mayer who turned film into a product and who saw it was essential to control the sale and distribution of films. The Americans have always seen film as a global business and the heart of the entertainment industry, but in Britain, like much of Europe, we have been preoccupied with the cultural and creative aspects of film-making, rather than the business of selling films to audiences. We have paid a high price in lost opportunities.

Unlike Hollywood, the British film industry has been hopelessly fragmented, comprising generally undercapitalised independent producers struggling to produce one film, and then concentrating on its production rather than marketing and distributing it. Of late, only Rank and EMI had their own cinema chains. Even progressive companies like Goldcrest, which retained the copyright to its film library, licensed distribution to others and so profits flowed to those distributors. Britain has lacked distributors with global reach, unlike the Hollywood studios, who can distribute films in a cost-effective way to cinemas around the world.

Too many uncommercial films have been produced, with too little time spent developing film scripts. Unlike Hollywood, where marketing budgets can be bigger than the production cost of the film, British film-makers have traditionally spent comparatively very little on marketing and distribution, in large part because they were operating on shoestring budgets in the first place. Until the mid 1970s, the typical marketing outlay for a British film was just 10% of its budget.

From Alexander Korda's Denham Studios in the 1930s to Ealing Studios, the production arms of Rank and EMI, and Goldcrest in the 1980s, they all enjoyed bursts of success and glory, attracted City finance, only to decline later and be deserted by the City. A cycle of boom and bust happened every decade. The main reason is unpalatable. British film-makers have tended to focus on creativity while US film-makers' primary interest has always been and continues to be making money.

A strong pool of British creative and technical talent continues to attract international film-makers. With leading post-production and technical support services, it has firm, if not always formal, links with partners in the US and Europe, and in recent years India. But independent film-making also requires strong management and disciplined financial and administrative skills, skills which are difficult to mix with creative flair and passion for celluloid.

The film industry has also been subject to economic cycles. Demand and supply of films as a product, and who controls and who has access to distribution are key structural issues that have always faced the British trade. With each decade it seems a small independent producer has struck gold, and on the back of a box-office hit, City funds have been attracted, only for the boom to turn to bust and disillusionment to set in among the investment community. With each slump, the US majors have strengthened their control and influence.

In reality, British film production has been a cottage industry, with small independent producers struggling to survive and, almost against the odds, occasionally producing a hit. The franchise model of mini studios with National Lottery funding and supervised by the Film Council may change this for the twenty-first century, but only if a more businesslike and international perspective is pursued. It is too early to tell whether this will succeed, and some may say it is too late anyway.

For most of the twentieth century, film-making has been a commodity business, where small independent producers have struggled to raise one-off finance for single films, deprived of distribution and having to sell the rights to raise the production finance. Structural weaknesses in the industry, with distribution controlled by Hollywood studios and exhibition dominated by the old Rank and ABC duopoly, and the lack of vertically integrated studios, have hampered the British film industry for most of the century. Alan Parker, the successful film director and now chairman of the Film Council, commented on this in a BBC radio interview during spring 2000: 'We have been making too many small films. If you make an aeroplane that flies too close to the ground, probably it is going to crash.'

At the end of the century when the industry is booming and for the first time we have a single funding body that can also invest directly into commercial films, the box-office hits have once again made way for disappointing productions like *Honest, Maybe Baby* and *Rancid Aluminium.*

The newsletter *Screen Finance* concludes that the industry is still characterised by a large number of films being produced by one-off production companies. Some 47% of the films made between 1995 and 1997 were by first-time directors, and 87% of those are yet to work on a second. For investors, such a fragmented structure makes investing in the British film industry 'a complete lottery' and unattractive to institutional investors, says Robert Padgett, head of private equity management at Hermes Investment Management, who invested in the Renaissance Film Company.

AMERICAN INFLUENCE

Hollywood's success and influence over the British film industry have been based on its control of distribution. It started in the early 1900s when Carl Laemmle, William Fox and others took control of American distribution and combined ownership of the studios with the cinemas, and it was consolidated after the First World War when they used distribution to control foreign markets, and then again in the late 1950s when their film libraries could be exploited again by selling television rights. It is therefore inevitable that British cinema has seen so many Hollywood films and that independent British producers have watched their films take second place on the big screen.

The UK film industry has been dominated by Hollywood and American feature films for most of the century. British audiences have been fed a diet of US culture. Hollywood studios have always had far greater financial resources to fund production, distribution and marketing budgets. Films like *Titanic* and *Saving Private Ryan* had huge marketing budgets and stimulated public awareness before the films were screened.

Britain, and especially London, has benefited intermittently from investment dollars and also attracted US film-makers to its technical talent and the post-production houses in Soho. This periodic investment has probably saved the film industry in Britain. So, however unequal the Hollywood and British film industries have been, Hollywood has needed the creative and technical talent in Britain, and domestic film producers have for too long been reliant on Hollywood's distribution and investment dollars. Inevitably, many films which are quintessentially British in humour or setting are financed by Hollywood; films like *A Fish Called Wanda*, *Sense and Sensibility*, *Emma*, *Hamlet* and *The English Patient*.

FUNDING

Quotas and subsidies do not have the desired effect. The Cinematograph Films Act 1927 was passed to protect the industry against American competition. By defining a quota of films that had to be British and which distributors and exhibitors had to meet, the issue became what was a British film. This issue was repeated with the Films Act 1985, and the definition of what is a British film has rested on financial rather than creative criteria.

Tax concessions have been exploited by financiers and only served to manipulate the market. But as shown in the 1980s with capital allowances and in the 1990s with sale and leaseback, film tax partnerships, and the Enterprise Investment Scheme, tax concessions are a proven stimulus for attracting investment finance into the film industry. Compared to Hollywood, even in the golden era of the late 1990s, the British film industry, which in many ways has been dependent on investment dollars from Hollywood, invests a fraction of Hollywood's annual $35 billion outlay in making American feature films.

Unlike the Hollywood studios, without vertically integrated groups and rich parent companies in the media and telecommunication sectors, British film investment has come from disparate sources, combining pre-sales of distribution rights, bank and bridging finance from banks specialising in the sector, sale and leaseback tax deals, national and local subsidies, and private investors. Now, as before, equity investment in film from the private sector plays a minor role. Specialist banks have included Hill Samuel, the media banking department of Coutts, Guinness Mahon, Barclays Bank and Credit Lyonnais as well as American banks. Credit Lyonnais was the first bank to lend seriously to the film industry when it backed Charles Pathé in the late 1890s, and is still very active today.

STRUCTURE AND DISTRIBUTION

The domestic film industry has for most of the century never operated in an open market, dominated by the cinema chains of ABPC (EMI) and Rank and then later by the television channels, including the IBA/IATA, the BBC and Channel 4.

Independent film producers are generally unsuccessful, as are the film production funds. Most independent film companies in the UK have been and continue to be undercapitalised, making too many low-budget films, and film finance has always been a critical issue. There have been too few integrated companies combining development, production and distribution. In its first report, published in May 2000, the Film Council lamented 'a failure to attract significant finance from the financial markets or key potential trade investors'. The distribution sector has never prioritised British films, and marketing budgets are too low and can rarely compete with the Hollywood studios.

It is hard not to conclude that Britain's independent film industry is no more than a cottage industry, punctuated by the occasional one-off success, which excites the industry into believing it can crack the American market, and then failing to live up to its own expectations. In contrast to Hollywood, and until the 1990s, the British film industry has been made up of small and undercapitalised companies who are either in production or distribution. Very few of these companies had their own studio. Hollywood is based around seven major companies which are involved in both production and distribution: MGM, Sony, Paramount, Universal, Warner Brothers, Walt Disney and Twentieth Century–Fox.

Hollywood has always regarded movies as a business, and just one part of a massive communications and media industry. This has attracted a wider pool of investors and created a climate where the film, television and video industries have mutual interests and coexist. The growth of the internet and telecommunication industries has created mergers with media groups, and as new distribution channels are created in the form of video-on-demand down telephone lines, the demand for film libraries has increased. Japanese electronics manufacturers like Sony, JVS and Matsushita have invested heavily in the film industry in America. Britain undoubtedly has the creative and technical talent. London is a hotbed of expertise for post-production, and the supply of technical talent attracts the Hollywood studios to produce their blockbusters in England.

Unlike Hollywood's studios that created what became hugely valuable film libraries, British film companies, including Rank and EMI, failed to build up film libraries because the industry did not develop large, well-capitalised companies capable of producing, marketing and retaining ownership of a portfolio of films over many years. The UK has always been fragmented; the exploitation of the rights to films has been ineffectively managed and all too frequently negotiated from a weak financial position, resulting in the distributors and cinema-owners consistently making the real money. Over the century, this fragmented structure has meant that too high a percentage of the box-office receipts has flowed overseas and usually back to Hollywood.

The fundamental problem for independent producers has always been, and continues to be, that major distributors are owned by foreign companies, and there has also been concentration among the cinema-owners. Now, in the twenty-first century, distribution and exhibition are dominated by American companies who will inevitably favour their own higher-budget movies. It will always be difficult for lower-budget, art-house and domestically orientated films to be shown. Even in the days when Rank was committed to independent producers, there was always pressure to show the latest Hollywood films.

The five major US distributors, each of which is owned by a major US film studio, took 82.9% of box-office revenues in 1998, up from 76.5% of box-office receipts in 1996 (Table 12.1). They distribute the films made by their parent companies, and their schedules are for the year ahead, which leaves little room for films of independent UK film-makers.

The independent distributors, who account for 63.5% of the films but only 17.1% of the box office in 1998, distribute mainly UK and continental films. New companies with significant financial

Table 12.1. *Leading distributors by number of films shown in the UK and percentage share of box-office receipts in 1998.*

	Number of films shown	Percent of all films	Percent of box office receipts
US majors			
Twentieth Century–Fox	17	5.2	25.2
UIP	36	10.9	23.2
Buena Vista	27	8.2	19.0
Warner	25	7.6	9.1
Columbia	15	4.6	6.4
Subtotal	120	36.5	82.9
Independent producers	209	63.5	17.1
Total	329	100.0	100.0

Source: *BFI Film and Television Handbook 2000,* based on figures supplied by A.C. Nielson, EDI, BFI, Screen Finance, X25 Partnership

resources are entering the market, but it will be many years before they can expect to become a serious challenge to the US majors, who will probably buy them out anyway unless the European Commission protects Europe's indigenous distribution channels.

In 1998 there were seven leading independent distributors: Entertainment, Polygram, Film Four, Pathé, First Independent, Artificial Eye and Alliance Atlantis. Entertainment and Polygram are the biggest independent film distributors with earnings of £45.4 million and £25.4 million, respectively, in 1998; Film Four earned just £5.3 million.

At the start of the twenty-first century and following closures including First Independent and Carlton Film Distributors (formerly Rank Film Distributors), and a spate of mergers, the major independent distributors are now Pathé, Icon Film Distributors, Redbus Films, Alliance Atlantis and Film Four. Alliance Atlantis is a Canadian company associated with the German company Kinowelt; Redbus Films is the vehicle of the internet multimillionaire Cliff Stanford, who founded and sold Demon Internet to Scottish Telecommunications for £66 million in 1998.

The concentration among cinema-owners has also hampered independent film production (Table 12.2). Odeon Cinemas Ltd was sold in February 2000 by the Rank Organisation to the City venture capital house Cinven, which already owned ABC Cinemas Ltd. United Cinemas International, Showcase and Warner Village Cinemas are all US-owned, and UGC Cinemas is France's largest cinema group, which acquired Virgin Cinemas in 1999. The largest six exhibitors together own only 34.6% of cinema sites but 72.8% of all cinema screens in the UK.

Table 12.3 puts the case for prioritising the distribution and exhibition of UK domestic films and making it the Film Council's principal objective. It contains disturbing statistics. In a decade when there is a resurgence in the UK film industry on the back of a number of box-office hits, the actual percentage of UK films gaining a release in the first year has fallen. According to its 2000 *Film and Television Handbook*, the BFI's explanation is that 'the distribution network for UK films has become fragmented'. Another reason is the continuing decline of art-house cinemas, which are found mainly in the south of England.

Table 12.2. *UK cinema operators by number of sites and screens in 2000.*

Company		Sites	Screens
Odeon Cinemas Ltd		75	464
ABC Cinemas Ltd		57	175
	Subtotal	132	639
UGC Cinemas Ltd (formerly Virgin Cinemas)		36	325
United Cinemas International UK Ltd		32	325
Warner Village Cinemas Ltd		33	300
National Amusements (Showcase)		17	200
Cine-UK Ltd		12	200
Smaller chains		75	104
Independents		420	640
	Total	757	2,733

Source: Key Note reports

Table 12.3. *Types of release in percentage terms for UK films, including co-productions, 1990–97.*

	Wide release	Limited release	Unreleased
1990	29.4	47.1	23.5
1991	32.2	37.3	30.5
1992	38.3	29.8	31.9
1993	25.4	22.4	52.2
1994	31.0	22.6	46.4
1995	23.1	34.6	42.3
1996	19.0	14.0	67.0
1997	15.5	19.0	68.5

Note: wide release covers films that were opening or playing on 30 or more screens around the country within a year of production. Limited release covers films that were released mainly in art-house cinemas or given a short West End run within a year of production

Source: *BFI Film and Television Handbook 2000*, based on figures supplied by Screen Finance, X25 Partnership, A.C. Nielson, EDI, BFI

The industry's biggest problem has always been the low proportion of films that are released to the cinema circuit. The Film
Council intends to address this issue, and the European Commission
has stated its support for film distribution in Europe. The monopolistic structure of the industry, which for so long was tolerated to
protect the Rank and ABPC duopoly has now been lost to the
Americans. The rationale was that the profits from their cinemas
funded their film production. But as the duopoly declined, the
Americans came to dominate the industry by default and benefit
from the tolerance to permit a monopolistic structure. But now big
American corporations have to deliver profits to their shareholders,
they have neither the inclination nor the sympathy to nurture British
home-grown talent, which many would argue is short-sighted when
some of those directors could be producing tomorrow's blockbusters.

PRACTICAL LESSONS

For investors there has been one simple statistic. One profitable film
has to finance ten that either break even or lose money. With those
odds, no wonder backing one-off productions has proved to be a
high-risk investment. As Hollywood has demonstrated so successfully, promoting a film, and advertising budgets, play a big part in
the film industry, and small advertising budgets have been a perennial problem for independent UK film producers.

For independent producers and investors, there are eight golden
rules:

1. Film finance is a high-risk business
2. Invest in a portfolio of movies, and treat it like a venture capital
   portfolio
3. Select the production and acting team very carefully and back
   proven talent
4. Never forget the luck factor
5. Distribution is key, so look for pre-sales to distributors and good
   sales agents
6. Never underestimate the difficulty of breaking into the American
   market

7. Production companies should develop sales arms to earn sales commissions on films they sell to distributors
8. Films, like any consumer product, needs to be sold; promotion and marketing budgets are essential

Directors and producers need to resolve the conflict between producing art-house films and commercial films. Generally, too much attention has been paid to creativity, and not enough attention and financial resources applied to marketing and distributing the finished product.

For government, the main lesson is clear. Tax concessions to ease the net cost of film production and a favourable tax regime to encourage foreign artists are just as important as providing subsidies to British film-makers. In fact, there is an argument to say that tax concessions in a market economy are more effective than providing subsidies, although a more balanced approach is to combine both, as is now happening.

The structure of the film industry needs to mirror the 'vertically integrated' and 'horizontally integrated' companies in Hollywood, combining the functions of a production studio, distributor and exhibitor, and extending horizontally into merchandising, publishing and computer games. Film finance should be a venture capital business supported by disciplined financial management which spreads the investment risk over a portfolio of films. Business sense should drive the business and at the same time allow the creative talents to produce innovative and interesting subjects. But there is the dilemma that has always faced the industry. Business skills and creative skills are not always good bedfellows, and few individuals combine both. So partnerships between creative and business talent are essential.

It may be an unpalatable fact for creative directors, but producing films is essentially akin to the venture capital business. It is high risk with a high failure rate, and with all the risk management and marketing techniques now available, success can still be random because of the 'X factor' of creativity and capturing the mood of audiences. So any investment should be spread across a number of film projects, in the knowledge that for every ten films made, one may be a box-office hit, two or three will do reasonably well, and the rest will fail commercially.

NEW TECHNOLOGIES

The impact of new technologies is typically greeted with caution and often underestimated. Just as Harry Warner in the 1920s considered the future for the talking movies was as a musical gimmick for impoverished theatre-owners, and the Hollywood studios initially feared the threat of television, so the advent of video-on-demand, cable and satellite TV, and DVD provides new challenges and opportunities for film producers and investors.

The simple fact is that there is an insatiable appetite for content. Cinema, video, terrestrial, cable and satellite TV, and now the latest technologies of DVD, all demand massive amounts of film to enable pay-TV to attract subscribers. There is no doubt that the huge growth of digital television and internet technology will bring new opportunities for the production and distribution of films. And we are talking on a global scale, where English is the *lingua franca* of the world.

Unless we leave the rigours of market forces to shape what is a grossly undercapitalised industry with distribution channels controlled by American and multinational companies, the industry will need financial incentives to attract investors and to train and develop the creative talent that is the bedrock for the future. The prize in the twentieth century was won by Hollywood. Let us not make the same mistakes in the twenty-first century.

CHAPTER 13

The Future

The twentieth century has ended and the new millennium has begun with a greater confidence in the UK film industry. Cinema audiences are increasing, with more multiplexes being built, and consumer spending on film and videos is forecast to remain strong. Terrestrial, cable and satellite television networks have a huge appetite for films, and this demand is attracting finance to help the film industry grow. A pan-European network of television, cable and internet organisations is forming and they will have an impact on Europe's film industry, both in terms of increased audiences and also increased investment in film production from those networks.

The combination of the Film Council and tax concessions show government support for the industry, with a tax regime that has never been so favourable. Providing the structure of the film industry can be addressed, it faces a comparatively bright future, although independent producers are still in the trap of seeking finance for one-off projects. In the late 1990s there were examples of successful producers securing funding for a series of films to spread the investment risk. The British Academy of Film and Television Arts (BAFTA) is changing the timing of its awards ceremony so it is before the American Academy Awards, the Oscars, a sign that the BAFTA awards are attracting more international attention.

Major film centres like India's Bollywood are looking for locations in the UK. With around 2 million Asians living in Britain, Indian film-makers have in recent years been attracted to the UK and notably Scotland. In 2000 ten Bollywood films were scheduled to have been made in Scotland, and more are expected; and the Scottish Film Studio Trust is expanding its film studios in Edinburgh. The net effect is that British film-makers should benefit. John Darke of the Office for National Statistics (ONS) expects audience figures to keep rising. In 2001 films like *Harry Potter and the Philosopher's Stone* and *The Lord of the Rings* have attracted children with their parents.

According to the Film Council, investment in British films in 2000 rose to a record level of £540 million, compared to £404 million in 1999, due partly to the production of the £75 million film *Harry Potter and the Philosopher's Stone*. Steve Norris, the British film commissioner, said that the weaker pound against the dollar and tax concessions had proven to be incentives in attracting foreign productions. But he warned that heavy global competition threatened the industry: 'Without the continued support from government in the form of tax breaks the incredible success we have seen this year may be short-lived' (*Financial Times*, 23 January 2001).

For Hollywood, the trend for blockbuster movies with big budgets and huge promotional campaigns will continue to produce sequels as 'film brands' are created, spinning off valuable merchandising revenues. Many of these films will be produced in the UK. The battle between business and creativity will continue and the 'creatives' will continue to lose out, unless and until they learn to exploit the film rights they are creating and retain control of ancillary distribution rights.

NEW TECHNOLOGIES

The growth of computer-generated imagery, digital television and internet technology and the demand for audio-visual entertainment will bring new opportunities for the production and distribution of films, and make film libraries ever more valuable.

New technology like DVD means films can be reversioned. Existing films can be edited in different ways. Discarded rushes from first releases can be re-edited to extend films. This enables producers and directors to recut and re-release films to new audiences. Steven Spielberg did this in 1981 with a special edition of his 1977 film *Close Encounters of the Third Kind*, and Francis Ford Coppola's 1979 war epic *Apocalypse Now* is being released in an expanded version. Warner Brothers have produced a DVD version of the 1959 classic

Ben Hur, which includes an informative documentary and screen tests with Charlton Heston commentating. With DVD the market for out-takes and alternate versions is expanding. But will this improve the original film versions from the filmgoers perspective?

Digitalisation means that images of old movies can be reused and, via computer graphics, new feature films created. Imagine seeing Marilyn Monroe and Michelle Pfeiffer together in the same film, or Clark Gable and Sean Connery. Video and now DVD will mean an increase in straight-to-video distribution deals. Broadcasters will play an increasing role in financing feature films as they can create valuable film catalogues.

Film specials and 'blockbusters' for television are getting bigger. In 2001 the children's book *Dinotopia* was filmed as a six-part miniseries by the American production house Hallmark Entertainment at Pinewood Studios with an $80 million budget and elaborate special effects. Other television movies include *Jack and the Beanstalk* and *Lost World*. These three projects illustrate the trend of 'event television' – made-for-TV drama on the same scale as feature films and intended to appeal to global audiences, with large production budgets, leading Hollywood talent and state-of-the-art computer animation. The BBC is producing *Lost World*, a two-part miniseries telling the story of a team of scientists in the Amazon discovering dinosaurs and apemen. Using computer animation for the dinosaurs, it will be the most expensive production the BBC has ever done.

To make these television films pay and justify an average cost of $5−8 million per hour of programming, the financing structure is almost as complex as a feature film. Distribution is via international media groups on a territory-by-territory basis; they are asked for similar pre-sales as a theatrical distributor in each country would have to contribute to the budget of a feature film. A huge project like *Dinotopia* is also financed via video sales and tax funding and one of the major US networks, in this case ABC. Event television is a growing trend, illustrating how the meaning of 'made for TV' is changing. The small screen is getting bigger.

New technologies also mean new intellectual rights that can be exploited by the producer. The increase in the number of channels which comes with digital technology and so-called portal TV over the internet is a huge opportunity for rights owners. In the 1990s global earnings from video sales and rental exceeded theatrical revenues, so the control of video rights has become increasingly important. Film producers need to ensure the revenues from new technologies flow directly back into the industry, and to do that they must control more of the sales and distribution of their films. For small operators, that will require forming alliances and strategic relationships, and this is already beginning to happen in the UK.

FINANCING TRENDS

Film financing will involve more commercial partners in Europe and the US. Merchandising and technology's capacity to 'version' films will add revenue streams to films. Branding and formula or character franchises will be created and exploited. New media rights, and for animation films, potentially lucrative merchandising rights, will be exploited. Copyright to small clips from films will be licensed in the same way as photographic archives of stills photographs are being exploited by Getty Media.

Product placement will grow, along with film sponsorship. In the biggest co-marketing deal in film history, Coca-Cola paid £95 million to the producers of *Harry Potter* for the right to use the film's logo on its cans in what will become a series of films; the first *Harry Potter* film cost £75 million. It went on general release in November 2001 and is expected to be shown on a thousand screens in the UK. Industry insiders expect the film to beat *Titanic* at the box office and to generate some £700 million in merchandising sales.

Film-makers are already turning to television talent to develop movie projects. As television companies are now big buyers and financiers of independent films, this trend will continue. We are likely to see interactive telephone rights, as first witnessed with Helen Fielding's *Bridget Jones's* film and books. The producers teamed up with Helsinki-based entertainment publisher Riot-E to provide an SMS text messaging service. Subscribers are asked to pay 10–15p a day for a few lines from her diary. They can also hook up to the 'Ask Bridget' service, which enables them to text Bridget for advice. Riot is targeting women in their twenties and thirties. This could earn the author an estimated £500,000 with a share of the telephone usage.

New technologies are creating new rights that mean the revenue-earning life of a film can now be much longer. We have already seen this with video rights and merchandising, and we will see it with DVD, video-on-demand and the internet. In the 1950s cinema box-office takings represented more than 90% of the film industry's revenues. By the 1990s, with television, video and merchandising, and allowing for increasing theatrical revenues worldwide, the proportion of revenue earned at the box office fell to 30%. With digital television allowing one satellite to transmit scores of channels, and other new methods of distributing films, commentators are predicting that by 2010 that proportion may drop to as low as 5%. But that does not mean mainstream cinema will become redundant. The big screen is and will remain the showcase for film product.

The convergence of entertainment and education is creating new opportunities for the film industry. Distance learning, or e-learning, is now becoming one of the growth global industries in the Information Age. English is the accepted *lingua franca* of the world (more than 90% of all electronic information is stored in English), and teaching English as a foreign language can be done in entertaining ways. The opportunities for the British film industry, and the exploitation of the different intellectual property rights in films, is very exciting in this multimedia revolution. As David Puttnam concludes in his book *The Undeclared War*:

> The balance of resources between Europe and the USA is very unlike the imbalance that exists in the traditional entertainment movie business. In Britain, for example, we are fortunate enough to have some of the world's finest talent in television and film production, in educational publishing, in animation and even in the authoring of electronic games. We have a unique range of relevant institutions, including the BBC, the world's premier public service broadcasting organisation, and the Open University, the world's most experienced distance learning organisation. ... Britain has the potential to become the 'Hollywood of Education'. (Puttnam 1997)

London is also a world centre for post-production facilities and technical expertise. Soho is heaving with companies that can edit, digitalise and create computer-generated characters.

For Britain's independent film industry to have a commercial future requires the support of American investment, which in turn requires tax incentives. American dominance over both distribution and exhibition, and also the video sale and rental markets, means that it is difficult for British films to be financed and shown. It is futile to try ignoring Hollywood's control over distribution.

US majors are happy to make films in the UK, but more reluctant to finance British companies. There are notable exceptions like the Bristol-based Aardman Animations, famous for its animated characters Wallace and Gromit and its first feature film, *Chicken Run*, which is being jointly released by Aardman with Steven Spielberg's Dreamworks SKG. It is the first of a five-film deal worth up to £170 million to Aardman. Independent producers have to rely on four funding bodies, British Screen, Channel 4 and ITV and the three licensees of the National Lottery. The onus is on those bodies not only to invest money in new films, but also to support that investment with management and marketing skills.

Tax concessions to the industry are proving to be a powerful catalyst for the industry, and Gordon Brown's 2001 Budget renewed his 1997 tax concessions for a further three years. John Woodward, chief executive of the Film Council, believes the tax breaks had generated approximately £500 million of film investment over a three-year period. 'Withdrawal of the measures would have been quite damaging,' he was quoted as saying in the *Financial Times* of 8 March 2001. Don Star of Grosvenor Park has been involved in financing more than 30 films in the last three years via film tax partnerships and sale and leaseback deals, and he sees the size of this market increasing. There are now some 40 countries that have co-production tax deals and the UK is party to most of them.

Tim Levy, chief executive of Future Film Group, a film financier, forecast that the decision would attract more investment from City institutions and predicted the emergence of new film studios, quoted on the stock market, within the next three years.

TELEVISION

The twentieth century ended with video and television being more important than cinema in terms of how audiences watch films.

Multichannel television gives audiences the choice of terrestrial network TV, cable and satellite TV. Viewers can watch what they want when they want, and for the BBC and ITV this means they now share a declining audience as viewers switch to movie and sports channels. In the 1980s ITV's target threshold was to attract at least 30% of the television audience; now it is 20% and falling.

Greg Dyke, the BBC's director general, wants to revolutionise British film-making in conjunction with Alan Yentob, the BBC's creative director. The £250 million venture will be the BBC's first foray into big-budget movies after decades of small-scale costume dramas. Funding is provided by MM Media Capital partners, a finance house based in Los Angeles and London which will oversee distribution of the movies. Formerly called Cobalt Media, which backed the *Bond* movie *The World is Not Enough* and Nick Park's animation film *Chicken Run*, the BBC hopes to combine private capital with its creative strengths and provide a platform to British film-makers without using licence fee funds.

Even before this announcement, the BBC had planned to spend around £8.5 million a year producing feature films. This is set to increase, and the BBC is creating new links with other bodies in the film and television industry. It has agreed with the British Film Institute (BFI) jointly to develop six new low-budget films from new talent; it is merging its Manchester production facilities with Granada Media Group's own Manchester-based operations; and it has agreed with Redbus Film Distribution to make eight films for distribution via Redbus, including video-on-demand rights.

But the BBC deal still depends on distribution, and the BBC and MM Media Capital do not have the backing of a heavyweight Hollywood distributor, so they are looking at how to deal with the big studios. Dyke aims to create a full-scale Hollywood-style film studio. In terms of using independent film-makers, he is on the record as saying that the corporation may struggle to meet its own 25% independent quota in 2001 because of the number of independent film companies that are merging with broadcasters, an issue which is of considerable concern to board members of the Producers Alliance for Cinema and Television (PACT).

Channel 4's film-making subsidiary, Film Four Ltd, had a budget of £36 million for 2000 to buy UK film rights, which is a 40% increase in funding. It has formed a joint venture with New Regency of the US, and with TFI, the French TV channel, to make *Queen Bess*, a film about the first Jewish Miss America. Film Four has agreed a long-term co-production and distribution deal with Warner Brothers Pictures, and its first film project is the $22 million film *Charlotte Gray*. Film Four is also working with European companies, producing an Anglo-German film, *Buffalo Studios*, set on a US army base in Germany.

THE FILM COUNCIL

The industry has high hopes of the new Film Council, which is one of the most important developments in the industry. Formally launched on 1 April 2000 and set up by the Department of Culture, Media and Sport, it brings into one organisation all the major publicly funded film finance institutions, including the BFI's film production department, British Screen and the British Film Commission (BFC). It has promised to take a more commercially minded approach to investing in British film, and it is responsible for six areas:

- The Arts Council of England's Lottery Film Department (temporarily renamed the Film Council Lottery Department)
- The BFI's production department (temporarily renamed the Film Council Production Department)
- Funding the production/development agency British Screen Finance and the British Screen European Fund
- Funding the BFI as a whole (which continues as an independent body)
- Funding regional film production activities
- The British Film Commission

The Film Council's budget is likely to be £55 million a year, derived from the Treasury and the National Lottery. Together with the BFI and the BFC, it will be involved in every aspect of the UK film industry, from funding and development to training, promotion and sales. Its aim is to help develop the UK's film industry and film culture.

The council's board is made up of the great and the good of the film and television worlds. The chairman is Alan Parker, the director of such critically acclaimed films as *Bugsy Malone, Midnight Express, Fame, Birdy, Mississippi Burning, Evita, The Commitments* and *Angela's Ashes*. Its chief executive is John Woodward, formerly a director of the British Film Institute and of PACT, which represents independent film producers and which he helped to found. Stuart Till, the council's deputy chairman, was formerly the chief executive of Polygram Filmed Entertainment and Universal Pictures International.

John Woodward's approach was reported in the *Financial Times* of 10 October 2000: 'We are trying to radically refocus the use of public funds to help build a sustainable British film industry. That means we are going to be more aggressive, more hard-nosed, and more objective than ever before. In the past, film policy has been run by civil servants – but that is going to change.'

In its first report, the Film Council identified many strengths and weaknesses of the UK film industry. Here are four major weaknesses:

- A failure to attract significant private investment
- An insufficient number of vertically integrated UK companies covering development, production and distribution
- A UK distribution and exhibition network which does not prioritise British films
- Too many undercapitalised production companies

The council's first proposals were announced in May 2000. Here are some of them:

- A major new film development fund with a budget of £5 million a year 'to support the development of a stream of high quality, innovative and commercially attractive screenplays'
- The Premiere Production Fund, with a budget of £10 million a year to facilitate the production of popular mainstream British films
- The Cinema Fund, with a budget of £5 million a year 'to back radical and experimental filmmakers, most especially new talent, and to explore new electronic production technologies'
- The Film Training Fund, with a budget of £1 million a year to support 'a massive expansion in training for scriptwriters and

development executives, and a tightly targeted programme to train business executives, producers and distributors operating in the international markets'

- Development of 'a comprehensive European strategy to expand business and creative relationships with European partners'. This includes earmarking 20% of each film fund for European-backed films (worth approximately £4.2 million a year)
- A programme to stimulate the export of British films and to exploit new opportunities in distribution via the internet
- A significant expansion of the British Film Office in Los Angeles to attract inward investment to the UK, promoting film exports and coordinating Film Council training initiatives
- First Movies, a National Lottery programme running in 2001 with a budget of £1 million 'to resource hundreds of low budget shorts offering children the opportunity to learn about filmmaking and display their talents'
- The creation of a market intelligence unit to provide authoritative statistics about the British film industry for the benefit of the industry itself, government and the media
- A package of 'specific measures to ensure that over time the British film industry reflects the rich cultural diversity of the UK, and offers equality of opportunity and access to individuals, whatever their background'
- A major review process 'aimed at creating a truly effective working partnership between the publicly-funded national and regional film bodies in the UK'

In early 2001 the Film Council announced further initiatives, including proposals to:

- Establish more favourable conditions to encourage the creation of integrated British film companies
- Facilitate access to venture capital and private equity and to address structural problems facing the industry
- Exploit the potential of new technologies

The Film Council's decision to channel some National Lottery funds into commercial film-making is a risky strategy. Typically, when a public body is combined with private finance, reaction to the Film

Council has been mixed. *Screen International* made favourable comments, and liked the notion that lottery money will not just go to artistic films but also to those that look assured of commercial success. PACT expressed mixed views, and in their own magazine in June 2000, PACT's head of film, Bertrand Moullier, made the following points. First, PACT wanted to see the £5 million development funding being spread 'across the whole spectrum of talent, rather than be tied down by long-term arrangements with a small number of companies.' Second, concerning the rules on partnership funding, independent film-makers 'should not be expected to bring the same proportion of private-sector capital as would be expected of an established film company.' Third, PACT questioned the quota of setting aside as much as 20% of the various funds for projects with European partners, and argued that a stronger European policy on the whole range of Film Council initiatives is needed.

PACT's main concern relating to film production is that the Film Council's approach to business affairs should be to increase the investment returns by incentivising domestic producers to retain key rights and designing a mechanism whereby revenues received by the Film Council from its equity investment are shared with the producers. This 'would help those with successful films put real money back into their development pot, rather than continue to depend primarily on lottery hand-outs in the long term.'

But critics question whether the Film Council can be any more successful than the Arts Council when granting lottery funds for film projects. Some question whether a public body should invest in films that have already secured partial funding from private sources, but that surely is to miss the point of a body whose primary mission is to be a catalyst for the domestic film industry. The concerns of UK distributors seem to be more justified in that they are not represented on the council, and that some members have links with Universal Pictures International, one of the major US distributors.

A three-year budget of £150 million is still small compared to the resources of Hollywood studios, so the Film Council has to initiate a coherent strategy for the film industry and support a structure with vertically and horizontally integrated studios. A number of dedicated film funds have been created, including a £10 million annual Premier Fund for commercial investment in at least ten mainstream films, and other budgets to nurture experimental film-makers, support screenplay development, and finance first-time directors using digital technology. The objective is to recoup the money spent by the Premier Fund over three to four years, which Tim Bevan, a member of the Film Council's board and co-chairman of Working Title Films, describes as 'totally unrealistic'. But John Woodward is determined to break away from the legacy of the Arts Council's terrible track record of investment when it supervised lottery hand-outs between 1996 and 2000, allocating £63 million. Only £8.7 million had been recouped by the end of 2000.

A smaller, £5 million annual New Cinema Fund will co-invest in more innovative films. Its goals will be more cultural than the Premier Fund, aiming at challenging audiences, developing new talent and helping artists working outside the mainstream of cinema. If there is a British *Blair Witch Project* that needs funding, then the New Cinema Fund will be there.

A third specialist fund is the £5 million annual Film Development Fund to support script development. A common fault in the past has been that independent films go into production too early, before the script has been refined with a vital third or fourth draft, because they need to start production to draw down cash to pay overheads. A minimum of 20% of each film fund will be allocated for co-investment with European partners.

The Film Council is expanding the British Film Office in Los Angeles to promote British films and to attract more US films to the UK for production. It will also promote co-financing and co-production deals between Hollywood studios and British film-makers. So the critical role of the Film Council is to build a sustainable structure for the British film industry. In the words of Tim Bevan, 'The end-game is that we should try to establish, within the next three to four years, at least three or four successful production companies like Working Title' (*Financial Times*, 10 October 2000).

Future initiatives will include contributing to the Film Industry Forum, set up by the Department of Culture, Media and Sport in 2000, which will be consulting with City financiers and distributors to discuss what changes can be made to support the British film trade in tangible ways. The high-profile role of the Film Council means it will inevitably attract close scrutiny and criticism.

INTERNATIONAL ALLIANCES

Alliances are being formed between investors, film agencies and producers and other commercial interests. Samuelson Films in early 2000 teamed up with BSkyB, WhiteCliff Film & Television and British Screen Finance (now part of the Film Council) to make low-budget digital films based on books written by Jan Brunvand, a professor of contemporary mythology at Utah University.

The film industry is also consolidating with the formation of a new giant international media group. In a $41 billion (including debt) merger in June 2000, French group Vivendi and its subsidiary Canal Plus merged with Seagram Incorporated and its subsidiary Universal Studios. Currently called Vivendi Universal, the new group combines US and European film production and distribution together with television, music and publishing interests and it plans to produce large-scale European movies. In the UK, Vivendi currently owns 22% of BSkyB, and in Germany Vivendi owns Babelsberg Film Studios. As the aim of any merger is to extract cost savings and exploit purchasing power, industry watchers expect cuts in their worldwide distribution network and major structural changes to the European film production and distribution industries.

In television, Granada Media Group acquired Anglia TV, HTV and Meridian, although the Competition Commission has directed that it must divest Meridian. This created the largest terrestrial commercial television operator in the UK and gives Granada immense buying power. After Channel 4 and the BBC, Granada has had a good record in supporting UK film-makers and in recent years has commissioned new feature films. In partnership with other companies, Granada has helped make films such as *Captain Jack*, *Essex Boys*, *Heart*, *The Misadventures of Margaret* and *Up on the Roof*. It has also been developing international partnerships to become a European producer and distributor of films.

CHANGING STRUCTURE

Ironically, after a history of backing commercial and critical failures, the last film supported by the Arts Council for England was the box-office hit *Billy Elliot*, co-financed by lottery funds and the BBC, and screened in the autumn of 2000. The consolidation of funding under the Film Council, and the council's commercial approach supported by lottery funding, bodes well for the future of the British film industry, especially if strategic alliances are formed with European and American distributors and studios.

Rank itself is focusing on gaming and leisure and divesting itself of its film-related interests, which J. Arthur Rank had developed in the 1930s. In 1997 Rank sold Rank Film Distributors, with a film library that included classics such as Laurence Olivier's *Hamlet* and David Lean's *Brief Encounter* to Carlton Communications, the media group. In February 2000 Rank sold its Odeon cinema chain to Cinven, a City development capital house, for £280 million. With 75 cinemas and 464 screens accounting for 20% of box-office sales in the UK, Odeon is the UK's largest chain. Cinven plans to merge Odeon with its 57 ABC cinemas, the sixth largest chain, with a 5.8% market share.

In April 2000 Pinewood Studios, the location for more than 700 films including the *James Bond* series, *Oliver Twist* and the *Carry On* comedies, was sold for £62 million by Rank to a management buy-in consortium led by Michael Grade, former chief executive of Channel 4, and backed by 3i, the venture capital group, and specialist lenders Intermediate Capital and Royal Bank of Scotland. Ivan Dunleavy, former head of VCI, the video and publishing group, became the new chief executive and declared that there were opportunities to increase Pinewood's share of the television production market. Within months it merged with Shepperton Studios and The Mill (its 40% owned special effects post-production business) creating a £120 million production company.

With Shepperton came the successful film director brothers Ridley and Tony Scott, whose credits include *Alien, Gladiators* and *Top Gun*. The plan is to expand the studio's television and feature film activities and compete in the global film production market. By merging the two leading production facilities in the UK, the combined group can compete with its European rivals, particularly in France and Germany. Candover Investments realised a £2.2 million profit on the deal.

In May 2000 the distribution sector saw Alliance Atlantis of Canada and Kinowelt of Germany set up a joint venture company called Momentum Pictures with the aim of creating a leading UK distributor. Cliff Stanford's Redbus, a new and high-profile distributor, has formed an alliance with Helkon Media of Germany and will distribute both US and European films in Europe. Redbus is also investing in films. Another joint venture has been formed between Metrodome Distribution and Future Film Group, a finance house, to buy films for distribution in the UK.

In June 2000 Filmgroup plc, which includes the Redbus film distribution company and aims to provide video-on-demand over the internet, pulled its planned £260 million flotation as stock market conditions deteriorated in the technology and media sectors. The appetite of institutional investors was diminishing at the same time as the Film Council was channelling funds into commercial films.

Channel 5 has emerged as the only independent commercial broadcaster to have a single majority shareholder, CLT-Ufa, the pan-European broadcaster which acquired Pearson's stake in the network. Channel 5 has established E5, a new division to develop digital channels and internet operations to complement its programming.

The rapidly expanding domestic and international television sectors are increasingly making existing UK and European regulatory structures unviable. The continuing existence of so many regulatory bodies such as the ITC, Oftel, the Broadcasting Standards Council, the DTI and the Office of Fair Trading, is now outdated, and the government is beginning to address this issue.

In a new age of multichannel television, video-on-demand, and portal TV on the internet, any new regulatory regime must address issues like access to the new media being not just confined to those who can afford it. The convergence of new media, including the transmission of films down telephone lines, means that the major discrepancies between European member states for licensing procedures and requirements need to be reviewed. Digitalisation of films also has social and cultural implications in terms of censorship.

The proven and successful Hollywood business model of vertical integration will be followed, and also horizontal integration where studios like Disney, MCA and Warner Brothers have expanded into international leisure companies. Generating revenue from 'books of films', music, merchandising, computer games and versioning scenes from films for e-learning will require media and educational business capacity.

SUCCESSES

Working Title have created a formula for success. A portfolio including *Four Weddings and a Funeral, Bean, Notting Hill, Billy Elliot, Captain Corelli's Mandolin, Bridget Jones's Diary* and *High Fidelity* has grossed more than $1.6 billion at the box office and secured 18 BAFTA award nominations. Its distribution deal with Universal and the subsequent $34 billion merger of Vivendi and Seagram (which owned Universal), with Canal Plus, the French television and movie business controlled by Vivendi, has been a happy coincidence for Working Title, as it merged Working Title's two main distributors.

Tim Bevan, co-chairman, reckons that in 2000 there were 20 producing units in the world that Hollywood considers viable, and Working Title is one of them. Its special relationship with Universal helps, as Universal underwrites its development and production costs and overheads. The marketing and distribution clout of a Hollywood studio is vital for international success. Perhaps it is because nothing succeeds like success, but Tim Bevan does not share many commentators' views about the sorry state of film-making in Britain. British film-makers need to think globally, he argues, which means creating a relationship with the mighty studios to distribute their product internationally.

Film production companies can become a brand in their own right, a brand which attracts talent. It happened with Goldcrest in the 1980s and with Working Title in the 1990s, where established directors and actors wanted to work with the company. New film brands will also be created. From the 1960s we witnessed Ian Fleming's James Bond become a multibillion-dollar franchise, and J.K. Rowling's Harry Potter looks like the next one, where sales from merchandising and video are likely to exceed box-office takings. Britain is also home to a successful and talented animation industry, and Aardman Animations, backed by Steven Spielberg's Dreamworks, will be creating families of characters that can lead to huge merchandising spin-offs.

We have the raw ingredients and talent for global success. Britain now needs the financial skills and investment, and the international distribution capability, to exploit that creative vision.

Glossary

above the line   the costs of acquiring the film rights and the fees paid to the scriptwriters, stars, producer and director; these are fixed costs as they are contracted

ancillary sales   sales that depend on the theatrical performance sales; they include TV, video rights, cable and satellite channels

below the line   the direct, day-to-day costs of making the film, including sets, costumes, accommodation, travel and wages, but excluding the acquisition of the film rights or the fees paid to the director, producer and leading actors

box-office receipts   cinema-owners retain 60% of the box-office takings, 15% goes in film prints and advertising, and the rest to the distributors; that leaves 25% for the distributor, who returns part of that to the film producer

capital turnover   the number of years it takes to turn investment into revenue; the Hollywood studios achieve an average of 1.5 years

completion guarantee or bond   a fee paid by independent film producers, it is like an insurance premium whereby the guarantor undertakes to pay all the costs above the agreed budget in order to guarantee completion and deliver the picture. The guarantor's fee is typically 6% of the budget, with a rebate clause that if the guarantee is not called, then half the fee is rebated to the producer. If the guarantee is called because of a budget overrun, production control passes from the producer to the guarantor, who is obliged to finish the film in accordance with the script

contingency   budgets contain a contingency of typically 10% of the below-the-line budget for cost overruns and unforeseen cost overages

contribution   balance of receipts after the initial film investment has been recouped, which is then available to pay for the general overheads of the producer

deficit financing   the gap between the film production cost and what rights have been pre-sold plus any guarantees from financiers or distributors; the gap can be funded on the back of the remaining rights to be sold and future profit shares

development   putting the film package together by securing the film rights, developing the script (and storyboard for an animation), selecting the director and principal actors, creating the budget, and finding production finance from third parties

distribution agreements   agreements entered into by the owner of a film regarding the commercial exploitation of a film throughout the world, such as agreements with licensors, licensees, sales agents and broadcasters

distribution fee   usually expressed as a percentage of film rental, a fee that covers the distributors costs

distribution finance   independent distributors (video, pay-cable, satellite, cinema distributors) who advance money for the production of a film in return for the distribution rights in their territory

distribution revenues   film rental less print and advertising costs, it is typically 25% of the box-office takings. From this the distributor pays out the film producer, and usually the proportion increases as the film generates more income. The distributor negotiates a similar sliding scale of income distribution with the cinema-owners

distributor   acts for the film producer, responsible for distributing the film to cinema-owners, printing and advertising, and collecting box-office receipts. Distributors play a pivotal role between the film-maker and cinema-owners; they determine which films are shown and for how long

exhibitors   cinema-owners

film markets   Cannes Film Festival, Milan and Los Angeles

film rental   typically 40% of the box-office takings, film rental is the receipts after the cinema-owners have taken their share

film rights   there are many different rights associated with a film that can be bought and sold as a feature film moves from its initial cinema release to cable, satellite and terrestrial television and to distribution on video and DVD. Separate rights cover each of these channels of distribution; *see* rights

forward sales same as a pre-sales (q.v.)

gross receipts box-office receipts are the cinema takings, from which the cinema-owners take typically 60%; a gross deal shares all box-office receipts between the exhibitors, the distributors and the producer

indirect costs includes contingency and completion fees

overage (1) the costs over the agreed budget; (2) the surplus revenue (back-end returns) after the distributors have recouped their advances and fees. Only commercially successful films return surplus revenue to a producer

packager a person who owns film rights and who packages the script, cast budget, director and funding. The packager takes the project to signing of contracts and the fund-raising stage, then appoints a line producer to handle the production of the film and the budget and schedule. The packager takes a fee and participates in any profits

pre-sales producers can pre-sell a film to a distributor on the basis of the script, the director, budget and cast. The distributor guarantees to buy the film at a certain price, payable on delivery or by instalments during the course of production. That guarantee may then be backed by a letter of credit from the distributor's bank, which the producers then use to get their own bank to provide film finance

producer packages the film and also controls the production of the film, including finances, contracts and logistics

production finance most production finance comes from cinemas, TV and video distributors, either direct via their production or co-production activities, or indirectly via distribution advances and guarantees

product placement branded products displayed in a film after the brand-owner has paid a fee; not all films pay for the privilege of displaying a known brand

profit participation developer, producer, director and stars share in the profits of the film. There is a difference in sharing in the net profit and participating in the gross. Gross participation is where defined profit shares are paid out before the investors have recouped their investment. Net profit is much less; it is the film rental less distributor fees and the print and advertising costs, and after the investors have recouped their finance plus interest

rights   the intellectual property rights to the original master sound and picture negatives of a film include a bundle of copyright rights that include territorial distribution rights, e.g. UK, US, overseas/ foreign rights; theatrical rights; videocassette sales and rental; television rights, including terrestrial, cable and satellite; network and syndication rights; digital TV rights; and internet rights. These rights can be in perpetuity, or for a fixed period of time after which the rights revert back to the producer or rights owner, and these ancillary rights can be sold again

sales income   money paid in advance by distributor networks, video networks or television networks for the right to distribute the film in certain territories

tax partnership   a partnership of investors buy a completed British film and lease it back to the producer, normally for a period of 15 years; the investors derive a tax relief on the purchase and the producer, as the seller of the film, realises capital to pay off any bridging finance raised to produce the film

Bibliography

Bardèche and Brasillach (1938) *History of the Film*. Translated and edited by Iris Barry. London: Allen & Unwin

Barr, Charles (1977) *Ealing Studios*. London: Cameron & Tayleur/David & Charles

Betts, Ernest (1974) *The Film Business*. London: George Allen & Unwin

Blue Book (1927–28) *The Theatre, Music Hall & Cinema Companies Blue Book*. Edited by T. G. Hatherill-Mynott. Redway, Mann & Co.

British Film Institute (2001) *The BFI Film and Television Handbook 2001*. London: BFI Publishing

Eberts, Jake and Ilott, Terry (1992) *My Indecision is Final*. London: Faber

Economic Intelligence Unit (1972) *Retail Business*, vol. 177.

George, Ken (1987) *Two Sixpennies Please*. London: Lewisham Local History Society

Hancock, D. (2000) Film production and distribution trends. *Screen Digest*, June

Hill, Derek (1959) Defence through FIDO. *Sight & Sound*, Summer/Autumn

Houston, Penelope (1963) England their England. *Sight & Sound*, Spring

Houston, Penelope (1970) Article on the Films Bill. *Sight & Sound*, Spring

Jackson, Michael (1980) Cinema versus television. *Sight & Sound*, Summer

Klingender, F.D. and Legg, S. (1937) *Money Behind the Screen*. London: Lawrence and Wishart

Low, Rachael (1949) *The History of the British Film 1906–1914*. London: George Allen & Unwin

Low, Rachael (1950) *The History of the British Film 1914–1918*. London: George Allen & Unwin

Low, Rachael (1971) *The History of the British Film 1918–1929*. London: George Allen & Unwin

Low, Rachael (1985) *Film Making in 1930s Britain*. London: George Allen & Unwin

Low, Rachael and Manvell, Roger (1948) *The History of the British Fim 1896–1906*. London: George Allen & Unwin

Macnab, Geoffrey (1993) *J Arthur Rank and the British Film Industry*. London: Routledge

Manvell, Roger (1955) *The Film and the Public*. Harmondsworth: Penguin

MMC (1995) *Report on the Supply of Films for Exhibition in Cinemas in the UK*. London: Monopolies and Mergers Commission

PEP (1952) *The British Film Industry*. London: Political and Economic Planning

PEP (1958) *The British Film Industry 1958*. London: Political and Economic Planning

Bibliography

Oakley, Charles (1964) *Where We Came In*. London: George Allen & Unwin

Palache Committee (1944) Tendencies to Monopoly in the Cinematograph Film Industry. London: HMSO

Puttnam, David (1997) *The Undeclared War*. London: HarperCollins

Selwood, Sara (1999) *The UK Cultural Sector: Profile and Policy Issues*. London: Office for National Statistics

Selwood, Sara (ed.) (2001) *The UK Cultural Sector: Profile and Policy Issues*. London: Policy Studies Institute

S.J. Berwin & Co. (2000) *Sale and Leaseback of British Films*, 2nd edn. S.J. Berwin & Co.

Spraos, John (1962) The *Decline of the Cinema*. London: George Allen & Unwin

Street, Sarah (1997) *British National Cinema*. London: Routledge

Taylor, A.J.P. (1965) *English History 1914–1945*. Oxford: Oxford University Press

Threadgall, Derek (1994) *Shepperton Studios: An Independent View*. London: BFI Publishing

Wakelin, Michael (1996) *J. Arthur Rank – The Man Behind the Gong*. Oxford: Lion Publishing

Index

Index

Index

Index

Index